CREATING SPECIAL EVENTS

DEDICATION

With this goal accomplished, I acknowledge with deep appreciation the loving encouragement, pride and devotion I have seen in the eyes of Don, Shari, David and Lee. In addition, these efforts are dedicated to my dear mother. She, too, made me believe I could do anything I set my mind to. And to my dad, who taught all seven of his children the value of CREATIVITY.

Creating Special Events © 1991 by Linda Surbeck, founder of Master of Ceremonies, Inc., headquartered in Louisville, Kentucky.

Published Spring, 1991 by Master Publications, Inc., 10323 Linn Station Road, Louisville, Kentucky 40223.

Library of Congress Number 91-90138

ISBN 0-9628820-0-3

Cover and illustrations by Jack Jeffries. Production assistance by Butler Book Publishing Services, Inc., Louisville, Kentucky

Printed in Canada

Creating
SPECIAL
EVENTS

By
LINDA SURBECK

1991 Master Publications

TABLE OF CONTENTS

PREFACE

Your interest in Special Events is well-founded. It is a tremendously exciting medium and industry. Special Events can cause unusual sales success for those who take advantage of their strength and wide range appeal.

This book, *Creating Special Events*, is one of the first books of its kind. It comes to you with the exciting answers to many of your "how-to" questions. It is my hope that these answers will effectively fulfill your promotional needs.

The idea for the business venture of special events management came to me after several negative experiences I had as a guest at some not-so-special corporate events. After witnessing a series of less-than-professional, image-tarnishing events, I was convinced that with creativity, energy and organizational skills, someone could step in and fill what was obviously a vacuum for professional management services... a niche!

However, when I set out to research the possibilities and educate myself in the specifics of professional events management, I found very little written on the subject. There was some information in magazines, and a few books in the advertising and public relations field, but no substantial information existed on the subject. Yet companies and organizations were spending millions of dollars to stage special events, and delegating responsibility for these events to an already overloaded and unqualified employee. I promised myself that when I was established in the business I would publish my experiences so that others could avoid the trouble I had trying to learn.

I initially found some information by visiting other special event firms in the more progressive cities around the country, gathering bits and pieces of information from some of the real pioneers in the business.

One company admitted that they allowed me some time because they were curious about me personally. They had postponed our appointment several times. Finally the day came and I had to call them to set the appointment back one hour. I told them I had been involved in an automobile accident the evening before, and would be coming as soon as I got out of the hospital. They tried to cancel, but I insisted I was on my way. Later, they confessed that they didn't really want to meet with me, but they "had to see this tenacious person!" I will always remember this lesson on the benefits of tenacity.

Armed with precious tidbits of know-how from some of these generous special events practitioners, I began creating the concept and building my own company by working twelve to eighteen hours a day; by believing all the positive input my very supportive family gave me; and by applying common sense, determination, creativity and energy to the development of operational procedures.

Another reason for writing this book is to publicize the value of the special events industry. I want to impress upon corporations, associations and organizations that there is a way to get a better return on their promotional investment in special events. My hope is that the information in these pages will show the business community that competition today *demands* that this critically important part of their promotion package be professionally managed either internally, or by a special events management firm.

Special events carry an implied promise — that they will be special. Special events are extremely demanding and delicate by their nature. They require creativity first and foremost, then experience to plan carefully, to organize and to execute. The chapters ahead will give you insights into this business through my personal experiences. This is only one way to proceed, but it has worked for me, and with application to your situation, it can assist you in the special events you may be planning. Read it thoroughly, but keep in mind that help is just a special events firm away.

As I stated earlier, I made a promise to myself, and to those who shared their knowledge with me, to share my experiences one day with those interested in learning the business of special events. That day has come, and I hope that this book may come to the rescue of everyone who is looking, as I did, for helpful information on this exciting industry, the professional management of special events.

Chapter
1

Defining the
Special Event

CHAPTER 1

DEFINING THE SPECIAL EVENT
What Are All These Celebrations About?

What exactly is a special event? And what makes it such an effective promotional tool?

An event is a happening — something that is created to bring people together for a particular purpose. Special means unusually good or extraordinary — something not to be missed.

A special event, then, is an *extraordinary happening*. It is a planned function with a distinct purpose, presented uniquely.

Special events are important parts of our lives, although we might not think of them as such. Consider the Academy Awards . . . the Tournament of Roses Parade . . . Mardi Gras . . . the Boston Marathon . . . the Kentucky Derby. These annual events have grown to such grand proportions that they have become national traditions as well as multi-million-dollar spectacles.

One-time special events can be just as memorable. Who can forget our Bicentennial Celebration in 1976, with its majestic tall ships and spectacular fireworks? Or think of the mega-success of the 1984 Los Angeles Olympic Games, or the Live Aid concerts for famine relief. Such events can, and do, capture the attention and imagination of the entire country — even the world.

Of course, not all special events are intended to reach such a large audience. Most are created to serve some specific promotional purpose — businesses sell products or services, politicians sell themselves, associations enlist members, and institutions solicit financial support.

There are many types of special events. A listing of the more obvious and popular follows. This list can also be a point of departure to create even more varied kinds of functions.

Table 1 Types of Special Events

GRAND OPENINGS
OPEN HOUSES
CONVENTIONS
SALES MEETINGS
FUND RAISERS
HOLIDAY EVENTS
FESTIVALS
CELEBRATION BANQUETS
PARADES
CHARITY BALLS
PICNICS
DINNER DANCES
COCKTAIL EVENTS
ANNIVERSARY CELEBRATIONS
THEATRICAL OPENING EVENTS
KICK-OFF OR OPENING EVENTS
SPORTING EVENTS AND TOURNAMENTS
SEMINARS
CORPORATE EVENTS
POLITICAL EVENTS
GROUNDBREAKINGS
STOCKHOLDER MEETINGS
PRODUCT PRESENTATIONS
CONCERTS
FAIRS
TRADE SHOWS
TOURS
SPOUSE PROGRAMS
THEMED GALAS
HOSPITALITY SUITES
RALLIES
FASHION SHOWS
COMMUNITY EVENTS
SALES EVENTS
EMPLOYEE HOLIDAY EVENTS
MOTIVATIONAL MEETINGS

Press Conferences

Many types of special events will be described in detail in separate chapters. But now you may be asking yourself: "What can the special event do? How can it benefit my business?"

Statistics reveal that hundreds of millions of dollars are spent by corporations on promotional events. In fact, special events have become an important segment of corporate America's overall marketing thrust, sharing companies' annual promotional spending. Why? Because special events carry a unique advantage, one that more conventional forms of advertising and public relations cannot match: the bringing together of buyer and seller in a relaxed atmosphere that accentuates the qualities of the seller.

This one-on-one, direct seller-to-buyer communication is the special event's greatest asset. It enables the seller to tell his story exactly as he wants it told, and to hear and respond directly to the needs of his customers. It enables him to direct his promotional dollars precisely to his targeted audience. The people who attend, after all, are there because they are interested in the host and have made a special effort to be there. They are curious, qualified and motivated.

Beyond this, what specific benefits can your organization reasonably expect to gain from a special event?

Business — whether measured in sales, profits, memberships, or funds raised. At the very least, you have communicated your best features to a highly motivated and qualified audience.

Market awareness and favorable name recognition — as you are associating your organizaton with a high-profile, enjoyable event.

Publicity — when a special event merits media attention — and yours can — it generates credible, objective news about your participation.

Loyalty — results naturally when your audience has accepted your hospitality and experienced your unique approach to business.

Employee productivity — is enhanced through such events as motivational sales meetings as well as social and family-oriented events like picnics and holiday celebrations.

Problem-solving — occurs spontaneously when decision-makers gather in a more relaxed setting where all the lines of communication are open.

Education and self-improvement — are central to many special events including sales meetings, trade shows and seminars.

Professional networking — the opportunity to develop business contacts with peers, colleagues, and even competitors, is a natural by-product of many events.

But is the special event a good idea for your organization? Would a special event be effective in accomplishing your particular goals? Would the considerable investment of time, money, planning and hard work yield tangible results?

Because of the excitement that invariably arises within any organization when a special event is being considered, it's prudent to step back and take the time to evaluate carefully and realistically both what you are putting into the event, and what you hope to get out of it.

Remember that a special event need not be extravagant and expensive. Events like the Olympics or the Rose Bowl Parade are for the heavy-duty investors who have calculated their investment return, and who have promotional budgets in the millions of dollars. Smaller companies with smaller budgets and more modest goals can scale down their investments and still produce an effective, memorable event, especially if they draw upon the ideas and resources of a creative professional special events manager.

The key to this issue is to approach the special event as you would any other business investment. Once the concept for your event is created and priced, it needs to be realistically evaluated. This may result in trimming one item here or substituting another there until the cost and the projected return come into positive balance. Like any public relations or promotional effort, the value of a special event is to some extent intangible, and its success will often depend on the expert judgment of someone who has experience with similar projects and who has seen their rewards months, even years after the event.

Special Events Research

As a first step toward creating an effective special event for your organization's needs, ask yourself these questions:

— What are the goals for the event?
— Who is the audience for the event?
— What promotional projects has the organization staged in the past? Which ones worked, and why?
— What kind of event will be the most effective?
— What kind of image should the event project?
— Is there an adequate budget?
— If the purpose is to gain publicity, is the event newsworthy by the standards of the local media?
— How many people will be necessary to organize and execute the event? Will they be available?
— Is the timing right, both within the organization and in the community?

If the results of your preliminary research indicate that a special project is in order, your next step is to determine the following:

— The manager of the event
— The location for the event
— The date for the event
— The message the event is to project
— The budget for the event

While each of these factors will be discussed in depth in later chapters, two points demand particular attention before committing to any special event:

The *choice of a manager* for your event is critical. If your organization has staged successful events before, you may be lucky enough to have someone in-house who possesses the qualities, energy, creativity, and time to produce the event for you. If not, you should at this point strongly consider seeking the services of a special events professional.

Related to the issue of who will manage the event, and equally critical, is *determining a budget.* It is always best to plan a realistic, rather than a bargain budget. For example, unless you can clearly afford $5,000 to $10,000, minimum, for an Open House for 200 people, you are better off waiting to stage your event until adequate money is available. Your audience — your guests, clients, customers, supporters — will assume that your special event reflects the manner in which you normally do business. Do not risk having an event unless you can do it right.

The chapters that follow will show you how to do it right.

Chapter
2

Creative
Brainstorming

CHAPTER 2

CREATIVE BRAINSTORMING
How to Invent the Outrageous

Now that you have decided to go ahead with your special event — and to do it right — the fun begins. It is time to be creative.

Creativity is *producing something new*. For the purpose of staging an event, creative equals special, and the specialness and success of your event will depend in large measure on the creativity you are able to bring to it.

But how does one go about "being creative?" How can you encourage and stimulate creativity among the people working with you on your event? We are all aware that the truly gifted individual — the artist — can produce something alone. But even the most creative person inevitably goes through dry spells when the ideas just won't come — and therein lies the danger of working alone, in a vacuum, depending on any single person for creative results.

A more effective method for developing new ideas is creative brainstorming, an approach that draws on the synergy of a team effort to produce results as good as, or better than, the creative genius working alone.

There are several methods of brainstorming being taught today by business consultants, but it is unlikely that anyone has improved on the technique used by Walt Disney and his creative team with such spectacular results. In this system, called *storyboarding*, every idea the group generates is written down on paper and the paper is put up on the walls. This way, nothing is lost or forgotten, and small, diverse ideas often combine into large, integrated concepts.

Disney called his team "Imagineers," and that is a great word to adopt to help motivate your brainstorming team. I have found that the most effective, creative team consists of just three people who share the qualities of clear thinking, self-confidence, and respect for others. These three should also be uninhibited, have good communications skills and the ability to think BIG.

The atmosphere of the brainstorming session should be spirited, enthusiastic and positive. Tolerance is also important. Competitiveness, threats, intimidation and fear have no place here. The group's attitude should be one of cooperation, teamwork, and fun.

Choose a room for your creative sessions that is quiet and devoid of intrusive, distracting elements. Telephones are taboo. Set aside sufficient blocks of time so that calls, meetings, and other demands can be handled later. Pads of paper and pens, comfortable seating, desks or tables, and a large erasable board are the team's only needs.

As you begin your brainstorming, try to employ these few general guidelines:

— Clear your mind
— Focus on objectives
— Think BIG and do not be restricted by whether or not something is "do-able"
— Say whatever comes to mind, initially only positive thoughts; save the negatives for later
— Search through your experiences for applicable ideas
— Talk only when you know you are contributing; do not interrupt the creative space of others

Everyone should have a copy of the results of your preliminary research (goals, audience, etc.), or this information may be written on the erasable board. Your organization's logo and colors should also be displayed. One member of the group, usually the one coordinating the event for your organization, will function as the team leader or moderator. This person's role is to guide the group along positive, productive paths, away from negative or irrelevant tangents.

Your first order of business is to come up with a specific goal for the special event — to describe as precisely as possible what you want the event to accomplish. Then ask yourselves, "When people leave this event, what underlying message should they take home with them?" Together, your event's goal and its message will provide the basis for the creation of an overall theme.

Depending on the nature of the event, you may wish to create an umbrella theme that will cover multiple events, serve as the focal point for the business year, or even be used for the company itself. Variations of the same theme, or related slogans, may be developed for various uses. For example, a company theme for Jones Manufacturing might be "Where Excellence Is Standard;" its theme for the upcoming business year, "Setting New Standards for Excellence." The slogan for a planned three-day conference becomes "The Gold Standard for Excellence," while individual events during the conference are sub-themed appropriately: "Golden Oldies," "A Gold Rush Gala," or "Going for the Gold."

Settling on a theme and sub-themes or slogans enables the brainstorming team to invent ideas for props, decor, costumes, food and event activities, all of which tie into the overall theme and each other. A list of areas that your brainstorming session should cover includes:

- Create a theme
- Create a slogan
- Conceptualize the promotion/event
- Design the invitation
- Develop an overall look for the event
- Design the decor, props, facade, lighting
- Create costuming or dress
- Create a clever overture to the press
- Create a special menu
- Consider special entertainment or speakers

Of course, it is never quite as easy as that. There are bound to be times or days when it is apparent to the whole team that those exciting new ideas just are not flowing. When you don't feel creative, you are not going to be creative, and so you should postpone the session until another day. This is not defeat — it is realism. It is natural and inevitable. Take a break and reconvene when everyone is feeling re-energized. Very often you will find that the seeds you plant one day will blossom overnight.

In the course of your creative brainstorming, negative ideas are certain to arise. As stated earlier, these negatives should be held back until the group's positive thinking has produced an overall theme and some solid ideas in each of the areas listed above.

Negatives — things that won't work or can't be done — serve to check the workability of your creative results. ("You can't put balloons on the Prudential Building because it's too tall.") Before sharing your team's ideas with the rest of the organizaton, you must be sure your concepts will work. A thorough, realistic self-critique of every element of your work will both save later embarrassment and help to ensure your event's success. Be sure to ask yourselves these questions:

— Is this idea new? Clever? Positive?
— Does it fit the organization's image?
— Will it in any way conflict with the organization's product, image, or service?
— Is it memorable?
— Is the overall theme rhythmical, so that it can be said easily and used elswhere?
— Do we love it?
— Are we proud of it?

If you have the right answers to these questions, then move on. If not, start reworking your ideas until you get them right. Often all it takes is a few simple modifications. Zeroing in on what is workable is very much a part of creating a concept that an organization can willingly adopt and successfully implement. Determining what will work depends on the budget you have to work with, the resources available, and the necessity of maintaining the desired image to be projected by the company and the event.

Working with the proper attitude of positive enthusiasm, cooperation, and fun, creative brainstorming can be extremely rewarding, even exhilarating. When your team hits on the right phrase or conceptual approach, you will know it right away. Good ideas, like laughter, are contagious, and the excitement they create is likely to generate still more ideas, bigger and better ideas. Polish the workable ones, discard the rest, and get ready to start transforming the results of your creative brainstorming into the reality of a unique special event.

Chapter
3

Organizing Your
Special Event

CHAPTER 3

ORGANIZING YOUR SPECIAL EVENT
Details on Mobilizing Myriads of Details

Organizing and staffing a special event demands someone with consummate personnel skills, because so much of the event's success depends on finding the right personality for each position of responsibility.

Usually, the decision to stage a special event has come directly from an organization's top management or public relations department. The sales or marketing department may have requested such an event, or an outside group that is putting on an event has solicited your company's sponsorship, and management feels it would be advantageous to get involved.

In the case of an association, the executive director, president or membership committee is usually the originator of the idea to have a special event.

In any case, whoever is at the top will necessarily delegate the real day-to-day responsibility for planning and executing the event to someone else, due to the tremendous volume of work and the multifaceted expertise required.

Seeking the services of a professional events coordinator at this point is highly recommended, especially if you are investing substantial money in your event, for the following reasons:

Time — If time sheets were kept on employees as they worked on a special event, the total wages paid would far exceed the management fee charged by a professional. Keep in mind that while valuable personnel plan the event, they are not handling their normal responsibilities for which they were hired.

Expertise — The in-house staff has specific areas in which they are trained, but very few are likely to have much experience in special events management. Putting someone in charge of the event without such experience increases the margin for error and greatly increases the chance that something will go seriously wrong.

Knowledge — Familiarity with the resources available locally (caterers, decorators, printers, etc.), established relations with providers of necessary services, and the ability to get the best value for your special events dollar, come from the volume and variety of work that a professional firm does routinely.

Attitude — Very often, the non-professional put in charge assumes that running an event is like throwing a fun party. With this frame of mind, that's exactly what you'll get — a party, not a business function designed to meet a specific objective, nor a return on your investment.

Creativity — This is the most important item to consider in the planning and execution of an event. Creative ideas lend an event its specialness, its indelibility. Usually, the in-house person selected to plan an event is a very thorough, detail-oriented individual, and while these are also important qualities, they cannot substitute for genuine creative flair.

If your organization is unable to hire a professional event coordinator, it is time to look in-house to find the best person to organize your event.

Usually, someone who reports directly to corporate management is the most likely candidate — and in fact the event manager should, at least for the duration, report directly to whoever has final decision-making and money-spending authority. What personal traits should this person possess?

— The ability to keep a cool head under pressure, and to instill this same attitude in other members of the event staff

— An outgoing, people-oriented personality — someone who can represent the organization during months of planning, smile constantly during the event and wave happily to all of the guests as they leave no matter how exhausted he or she may be
— A healthy body and mind; the ability to generate energy and enthusiasm from start to finish despite frustration and fatigue
— Creativity, of course. Creativity is an absolute must for the event's concept development, the theme, the invitation, the message, the decorations, the design of the event facility, and directing the work of the caterer and all hired services throughout the planning and execution
— A working knowledge of public relations: how to stimulate the interest of the news media so that your organization receives the publicity it wants and deserves
— Resourcefulness; how to find whatever is needed, especially if it's something no one has ever heard of or seen before
— Motivational skills to get the most out of tired people who have never done this kind of work before; to increase the staff's confidence in its ability to handle its responsibilities; and to show them how much fun working overtime can be
— Thoroughness and attention to detail
— The ability to understand financial matters and to keep an event within its established budget
— A knowledge of printing, especially the ability to handle printers and get them to meet deadlines
— A sense of theatrics, a flair for putting the drama into an event

Admittedly, it may well be impossible to find someone within your organization who possesses each and every one of these skills and qualities, but knowing the traits an event manager should have will help you to choose the very best person available for the job. And it will also help your event manager select the people to serve as the support team for your event, since their unique abilities may be able to fill in some of the gaps.

The Support Team and Its Responsibilities

Your special event requires special people for its support team. These are the people who supply the work and the energy that will make or break your event.

When selecting these "volunteers," be aware that their personalities will need to blend together and they will have to be able to work compatibly with the event manager. Generally, you are looking for people who can be described as:

- Creative
- Energetic
- Thorough
- Organized
- Resourceful
- Level-headed
- Supportive
- Image-conscious
- Promotion-minded
- Communicative
- Budget-oriented
- People-oriented

In addition to these general qualities, you'll want to find people who can contribute the following specific skills:

- Art/graphic design
- Publicity/media relations
- Print production
- Entertainment (theater, lighting, sound, stage direction, music)
- Copywriting
- Fund-raising
- Protocol
- Vendor relations
- Food service

But above all, and more important than any other characteristic or specific skill, is a positive attitude — a belief that no matter what the obstacles, the job can still be accomplished.

Every special event involves an enormous amount of work, and every event brings with it pressures and problems that can only be overcome if the support team is able to generate positive solutions. Some of the personalities hired to provide special services may be difficult and temperamental. Deadlines are a constant source of pressure. Large amounts of money must be spent wisely, not squandered. Changes at the last minute are the rule, not the exception. Fatigue catches up with everyone as the strain of late hours and lost weekends begins to take its toll.

The team leader will have the task of keeping the support team positive and productive, as well as being able to lead and communicate effectively, to compliment and cajole, to push and prod, to stimulate and most of all to motivate team members to continue giving their best. Remember that the guests attending your event will not be aware of all the painstaking effort that went into it, nor should they. What they see, however, will be a direct reflection of how well your team has worked together to accomplish its goals, which in turn reflects on the organization's management and its manner of doing business.

With all this in mind, what specific responsibilities and items must the support team handle?

— Setting objectives
— Determining the date and time of the event
— Developing a guest list
— Designing a creative concept
— Developing a budget
— Working with a designer and printer on invitations
— Hiring necessary services
— Purchasing items needed, including mementos
— Getting signs made
— Working with a decorator to develop a setting
— Designing special effects
— Working with various technicians (sound and lights)
— Communicating with vendors on a daily basis

— Developing a schedule for the day of the event
— Managing the event itself
— Doing a follow-up critique
— Approving and paying bills

Now let's take a clear look at the specifics involved in handling each of these jobs.

Setting Objectives

This is the first item that the event manager and support team must decide. For the sake of discussion, let us say that the team is planning a Grand Opening. The obvious goal will be to maximize awareness of the organization. However, during this first session, the team should discuss other possible advantages to be gained from its efforts. One-on-one communication with local officials, potential customers, and employees and their families is a good example. Positive publicity, making a good first impression, and developing customer loyalty are but a few more of the many possible benefits of your event. Think of it as a "show-and-tell" to introduce your organization and its products and services to the world.

Setting the Date

Again, using a Grand Opening as our example, your first consideration when setting the event date is the completion of your new facility. Taking the month it is scheduled to be ready as your target, check the calendars of your anticipated VIP's (company officials and local dignitaries), the firm's business production schedule, and the availability of needed vendors and service providers. Be careful to avoid holidays and conflicts with other community events. Also avoid Fridays, Saturdays, and Sundays in order to maximize the likelihood that local dignitaries will be able to attend. Generally, Tuesdays and Thursdays are your best bets, since most other types of business and organization meetings are held on Mondays and Wednesdays. But the best day will be determined primarily by the schedule of your business and the schedule of your guests, the point being to maximize attendance.

The Guest List

Your objectives will determine your guest list. First, consider those who have a vested interest in the organization: stockholders, various levels of management, bankers and others in the community who have assisted in this venture. Community leaders (government, church, civic, business, etc.) lend credibility to the image you are trying to project and may attract others. Current and potential suppliers should be included in order to gain their loyalty and future cooperation. Of course, the press must be invited for publicity purposes, and management may also wish to invite the company's employees and their families.

Naturally, some grand openings, as well as certain other types of events, are intended for the general public — your customers. These may be reached through direct mail, or through various types of advertising and publicity which will be detailed in a later chapter.

Designing a Creative Concept

The purpose of designing a creative concept is to make your event unusual — to get it talked about, to get media coverage and to make it memorable.

A creative concept is like a road map. It makes a strong statement to your guests about the purpose and intention of your organization, and it serves as a guideline in developing the specifics of the event for your event team. Use the techniques described in the chapter on "Creative Brainstorming" to develop a concept that summarizes the image for the company you want your event to project.

Developing a Budget

Your organization's management has probably already indicated how much they are willing to spend on the event. Once you have developed your creative concept, you will be able to begin costing it out to see whether or not it fits the constraints of the available budget. Occasionally this means cutting back on a few of your great ideas and finding less costly ways of doing some things. Itemize all your needs first, then develop a "menu" of possibilities and enhancements. You will soon see what you'll be able to accomplish within the budget. The important ingredient here is to think creatively in order to come up with less expensive ways to accomplish your purposes.

Working with a Designer and Printer on Invitations

Your printed invitation is the first indicator of both the type of event you are hosting and the way in which your organization conducts its business. It is often the very first impression of your firm that many people will receive.

Working creatively with a graphic designer will produce a memorable invitation. A professional designer can not only create a great idea for the invitation itself, but can also suggest ways to stretch your printing dollar. If no one on the event team is familiar with print production, ask your designer to work with the printer from concept through finished product. Often the designer is familiar with local printers and will be able to recommend the best and most economical printer for the job.

Other printed pieces you may need to develop — also with the help of the graphic designer — include name tags, napkins, promotional pieces, tour routes, RSVP cards, and maps.

Hiring the Necessary Services

Dealing with the caterer, photographer, rental equipment company, light and sound technicians, sign painter, decorator, entertainers, and other service vendors needed for your event requires calling, interviewing, and endless negotiating.

You need to get at least three bids on most services in order to obtain the best value for your money. Contracts must be carefully written and signed with each vendor, and letters of expectation stating all understood requirements should be sent to each as well. Send extra copies to be signed and returned for your files.

Purchasing Items Needed

It's shopping time! Linens, specialty gifts, decor and guest registers are just a few of the items you'll probably need for your event. Bear in mind that personalized mementos and other custom items should be ordered at least eight weeks in advance. Comparison shop, just as you would at the grocery store, in order to find the best value on every item, but always remember that you are looking for the unusual and unique that will help make your event truly out-of-the-ordinary.

Getting Your Signs Made

Signs tell your guests why you have "gathered them here today." This seems so simple and obvious that it is easy to overlook.

I once attended a promotional open house intended to sell space in a new office building. When I arrived, there was no sign to indicate that I was indeed in the right place. Although the function was being held on the third floor, no signs directed arrivals there. There were no signs to indicate which areas were available for lease, and no informative signs to help sell the space, its advantages, and costs. And since the event's hosts were too busy serving as bartenders to do any selling themselves, the whole purpose of the event was lost.

Plan your signage from the beginning to the end of an event as if you were the not-yet-informed guest. Start with the road(s) leading to the event site, and then develop a sign system designating each strategic area you want your guests to know about or move through. You have only a few seconds of their time to communicate the necessary information, so do it effectively through color, readable type and other design elements. Your printer may be able to help, or you may need the services of a professional sign painter. But in either case, signs are a small investment that can produce a large return.

Developing the Decor

First impressions are lasting, so the immediate visual impact of your event site on the guests is important. This first step will establish their expectations of the entire event. Use this opportunity to get them excited about what's coming before it even begins — a technique I call "programming from a distance."

Early in the developmental stages of your event, interview at least three prospective decorators, and when you have selected one, go together to the event site. You will need to measure available space, and to discuss your overall concept, theme, corporate image objective and major visual concerns, such as colors.

Once you have communicated your approach to the decorator, he or she will be thinking of appropriate props already on hand which will save you the cost of building new ones, and mentally taking an inventory of ideas and materials necessary to produce the look you desire. Take advantage of your decorator's professional creativity while at the same time making sure his or her ideas coincide with the event concept. He or she will have knowledge of new and unusual items — fabrics, paints, sets, lights, props — that can make your event look state-of-the-art. This is especially true of a professional event management firm.

Your objective in planning the decor is to create a memory that makes people talk about your event long after they have gone. I once prepared a "wish list" to give to a decorator for an event that I wanted to be the ultimate. This list included all the various emotions I wanted the event to evoke — delight, surprise, wonder, etc. — as well as the physical elements of movement, sound, and light. It suggested the use of such unusual items as butterflies, fireworks, bubbles, scents, and music-box sounds in odd places.

The results were fabulous. Unleashed from traditional approaches, my decorator was motivated to perform like never before. My list had provided him with a wide range of possibilities. I strongly suggest you use your own decor "wish list," which will allow your decorator's imagination and creative expertise to run free.

Of course, in this case I also provided the decorator with a great budget, which always helps. But don't let monetary constraints inhibit your creative drive or your vision of what your event could be. Always begin by planning and designing what you really want — then whittle it down to what is affordable. If you go into your event thinking small, that is what you'll get: a small, inexpensive-looking event. You want the event to convey to guests the message that your organization will always treat them in a first-class manner.

Decor is among the most essential elements of your event. Do it with as much style and class as you can possibly afford.

The following is a list created to stir your creative imagination when decorating for your special event:

Table 2 Decor ideas

Greenery	Mirror Balls
Flowers	Air Tubes
Crystal	Sticks
Water	Antique Elements
Glitter	Musical Instruments
Ice	Mylar Sheets
Lights	Buttons
Wood	Papers
Glow Lights	Spanish Moss
Wire	Car Parts
Tiers	Books, all types
Revolving Stage	Rocks
Fabrics	Trees
Table Linen Designs	Food
Balloons	Animals
Ribbon, varying lengths	Mobiles
Metallic or Glitter Ribbon	People
Chicken Wire	Mannequins
Petals	Props
Jewels/Gems	Art
Mirrors	Fountains
Fireworks	Iron Fences
Papier Maché	Fabric Sculpture
Sculptures	Baskets
Toys	Candles/Candlesticks
Surprise Elements	Plexiglass Tubes
Round Tables	Plexiglass Pieces
Bottles	Brass Containers

Table 2 continued

Silver Containers	Butterflies
Packing Material	Styrofoam Shapes
Bubbles	Giant Glass Bulbs
Popcorn	Paints
Video Projections	Shredded Mylar
Tubular Neon	Sheets
Tallow	Moss
Music	Electronic Parts
Motion/Movement	Fans
Tools	Carpet
Soundscape	Posters

Communicating with Vendors

"Communication" has become a buzzword, almost a cliché. But without real communication, misunderstandings can and do occur, despite best intentions. Nowhere is this more true than in the special events business.

Vendors — the people you hire to perform the many services necessary to conduct your event — are all just as busy as you are. In other words, it is likely that one of you will become distracted, even during an important meeting or phone call. You must take the time to listen very carefully to what your vendors say they will provide for the agreed-upon price — and make sure the vendor understands what points are important to you.

For example, for the concept "A Golden Opportunity," I wanted a ballroom to "turn to gold." For this effect, I requested that a giant pot of gold be constructed with gold coins spilling over the sides and golden lights radiating from the top of the pot up to the ceiling. In our final discussion before the event with my trusted decorator, I re-emphasized that I wanted everything to be gold, to which he replied, "Fine — a black pot with gold coming out" — no doubt recalling his childhood image of the traditional leprechaun's treasure. "No," I said,

"A gold pot of gold." I felt very strongly that every element of the set, including the pot, should be gold. Because the decorator had his own vision, we needed to put these thoughts on paper. If not for our final "run through," a problem would have occurred.

Well, I got my gold pot. But upon arriving at the site just prior to the event, I was puzzled to see two grey doors leading into what was supposed to be a "vault of gold." My vision of a vault of gold had — you guessed it — doors of gold. "Wait a minute," I said to one of the decorator's assistants. "When do these doors get painted? Do you have time?" The answer was "They have been!" My decorator had envisioned a typical, realistic vault with grey doors. But because I had failed to communicate my vision, we were forced that day to go with unexciting grey doors.

When discussing your plans with vendors, be sure to write down, in detail, everything you agree upon. Carefully examine this list for possible changes and embellishments you want to add while you still can, including any details or descriptive words that will make your wishes clearer (like the word "gold"). And make doubly sure to write down the price agreed upon for each item and service. I once hired a calligrapher to address invitations at a price I understood to be $1.00 per envelope, averaging three lines per envelope. Not until I received his bill for $1,300 more than I expected did I realize that his price was $1.00 per line. The real problem, of course, was that neither of us had put our understanding in writing, with the result that we both misunderstood.

Personal appearance is another important area of communication and understanding with vendors who will be present at your event. This is another lesson I learned the hard way. Having requested that a caterer provide "uniformed service people" for an event, I felt sure that I would be getting elegant servers attired in black and white. What I got was pink and brown — and since I hadn't specified exactly that I wanted black and white uniforms, the caterer was perfectly correct in thinking he had fulfilled my request. Unfortunately, their "uniforms" happened to be pink and brown.

On another occasion, I hired a man to serve as a "greeting gentleman,"welcoming guests and taking their coats as they arrived at the elegant mansion rented for the event. We had him fitted for a beautiful tuxedo — which we paid for — and he looked great and seemed to be doing a wonderful job. It wasn't until the evening was half over — meaning he had already greeted and been seen by every single guest — that I looked down, discovering to my horror that the man was wearing brown corduroy house slippers!

Details, details. Spell out in writing everything you believe is important in a letter of understanding. Much of your contact with vendors will necessarily be by telephone; however, be sure to document immediately any changes you discuss, writing down the date, the reason, and the name of the person you discussed them with. Do not trust anything so important to memory — either yours or the vendor's. And make sure that your staff or committee members follow the same practice.

Some vendors will send their own contracts for you to sign — this is for the protection of both parties and can also aid in your mutual understanding. But don't let it substitute for your own letter of understanding — the one that covers what is important to you.

Developing a Schedule for the Day of the Event

You will need to develop two distinct schedules for the day of your event. The first is a pre-event schedule for you and your event management team; this is a blueprint designed to ensure that the event comes off just the way it was planned.

To create such a blueprint, itemize every single element, including the time it should occur, the event team member responsible for it, the vendor involved and his or her phone number. Part of such a schedule might look like this:

Table 3 Event Schedule

Action	Time	Event Rep.	Service	Service Rep.	Phone
Management Team Arrives	8:00 am	Don	Master of Ceremonies	Shari	555-3021
Assume Rental of Facility	8:45 am	Margie	The Hotel	Eddie	555-2042
Arrival of Rentals	9:00 am	David	A-1 Rentals	Dick	555-1000
Decorator Arrives	9:15 am	Autumn	Decor Designs	Clint	555-6600
Musicians Set Up	12:30 pm	Lee	The Monkies	Lisa	555-0724
Balloon Arrival	1:15 pm	Paul	Balloons or Bust	Amber	555-2314
Caterer Arrival	3:00 pm	Sylvia	Fancy Foods	Ed	321-8040
Lighting Techs Arrive	3:30 pm	Roscoe	Heavenly Lights	Esther	800-5029

This plan for the day enables you to keep close tabs on every aspect of the event preparation as it happens, making sure that each step is completed on time. If a vendor has not appeared within fifteen minutes of the expected arrival time, call the service representative and make sure you do not have a problem — or begin fixing the problem you obviously have!

Be sure to allow a safety margin for the completion of your set-up of at least one hour before the event. This gives you half an hour for finishing up with late vendors and half an hour for details, touch-ups, and early guests. And give yourself time to clean up and refresh yourself so that you can manage the event looking and feeling relaxed and at your best.

The second schedule you will need is an agenda which details everything that is to happen from the minute the event begins, through its every step, up to and including guest departure, vendor clean-up, and departure of the management team. Spell everything out. Remember that this agenda will go to your organization's top management for approval. The more detailed and complete your agenda, the less your chances of having to make last-minute changes and cause the feelings of panic that last-minute scrambling usually creates.

Managing the Event

Ideally, this should be a piece of cake. You have planned every detail thoroughly, considered all potential problems and eliminated them, communicated with vendors and upper management, outlined every element and know exactly what is supposed to happen and when. Now all you have to do is get out of bed with a positive attitude on the event day, get to the event site early, have your pre-event schedule in hand, and check off every item as it happens. You are in control.

When your guests begin to arrive, put away your pre-event schedule and bring out your event agenda. The most important single consideration now is to coordinate all the activities by keeping them on time — even a 15-minute overrun in one area can complicate the whole event's agenda.

Your event management team can keep track of various activities by "stalking" the event. Spread out — unobtrusively — and try to look at things the way your guests are seeing them. Watch for clutter, trash, spills — anything that looks less than ideal. Go immediately to the source (vendor representative, or event team member) to get any problems solved.

Remember as you circulate that you are representing your business or organization (and are probably wearing a name tag that says so). Your smile and your demeanor should communicate to your guests, "We're glad you're here, we're trying our best to please you — and this attitude will carry over into the way we do business with you."

Your vendors also need to be kept happy — so they will stay on the job, and their attitude will help communicate this same message. They should know that they are responsible for cleaning up after the event. But if for any reason you and your team find yourselves alone after the event and there is still cleaning to do — do it. You are the responsible party, and you are the one who will have to answer to management for trash left behind and deposits not refunded.

Once clean-up is complete, of course, you're free to get into your car, drive home, walk into the bedroom . . . and collapse.

Critique

A critique session following your event is invaluable in determining how well you accomplished your goals. Some questions your team should ask itself:

— Did you get your message across the way you intended?
— Did you enhance your organization's image?
— Will your organization benefit from the event? How?
— Can you project the return on your investment?
— Do you want to have a similar event again? When?

These are the big questions, the answers to which will determine the overall success of your event. Now take a look at the details. What improvements would you make in planning this event again next year?

— Would you use the same or different vendors?
— Was the theme effective?
— Was the concept good?
— Go over every item on your original plan for the event and ask, was it effective? Could it have been better? How?

For large and/or complex events, it is a good idea to record your critique session on tape and keep this on file with the other records from the event. This is extremely helpful when it comes time to plan the next event as it enables you to recall precisely what the last one was really like — both the factual details and the emotional reactions of those involved. For smaller events, detailed written notes of the critique should suffice — and again, be sure to keep these on file for future reference.

Table 3 Event Evaluation Form

Evaluation Questions

	Yes	No

Were your goals identified and realized?

Did the concept accomplish the image you
wished to project?

Was it effective in reaching your targeted
group?

Was the event well organized?

Was the response from attendees favorable?

Did you feel attendees actively participated?

Was transportation satisfactory?

Did the location suit your needs?

Was the food presentation good?

Would you use this caterer again?

Was the lighting/sound system adequate?

Did the committees work well together and/or with
your event management firm?

What elements do you feel were most important?

What will you eliminate?

Committee comments:

Approval and Payment of Bills

The event is over. You feel it was special — your goals were achieved — and the message your guests took away was the one you intended.

Now you get to pay for it.

Many vendors require deposits upon signing a contract, with the balance due upon completion of the event. This makes for fairly simple bookkeeping; when the vendor sends a statement or invoice for the balance due following the event, just match it against the amount you negotiated in the beginning and write or request a check for payment.

If there is a discrepancy between what the vendor is charging and what you agreed to pay, it is up to you — not the accounting department — to clear up the difference.

The sooner you get the payment process behind you, the better your memory of the event will be. When you have finally gotten the last bill paid, you're done! Celebrate! Be proud!

Tools of the Trade

An event planner should have a tool box which includes (but is not limited to):

Scissors
Packing knife
Masking tape
Double-sided tape
Cellophane tape
Paper clips (large and small)
Stapler and staples
Small hammer
Small screwdriver
Assortment of nails
Measuring tape
Spot remover
Regular glue and superhold

Chalk and eraser
Pointer
Clear nail polish (for mending)
Cassette tape and recorder
Batteries
Long extension cord
Phone message pads
Small camera
Film
Flash cubes or flash attachment
Extra audio visual needs:
- light bulbs
- carousel tray
- splicing tape
- blank transparencies

Typing white-out
Safety pins and straight pins
First aid kit
Sponge
Handi-Wipes
Thread and needles
Extra mailing labels
Extra name tags
Cash box and change
Pushpins and thumbtacks
Throat lozenges for the speaker
Stopwatch
Rubber bands
String or twine
Plain 8-1/2" x 11" paper
Flashlight
Black bow tie — just in case!

Types and Examples of Special Events

As a special events practitioner, you should strive to produce unusual, unique and extraordinary special events. You can apply the skills discussed earlier in this book to any wild and crazy idea that comes your way. But, typically, you will be faced with the more traditional forms of special events. We listed many of the common ones earlier; here they are again:

Groundbreakings
Grand Openings
Open Houses
Conventions
Sales Meetings
Fund Raisers
Holiday Events
Festivals
Celebration Banquets
Parades
Charity Balls
Picnics
Dinner/Dances
Cocktail Events
Anniversary Celebrations
Theatrical Opening Events
Kick-Off or Opening Events
Sporting Events and Tournaments
Corporate Events
Political Events
Stockholder Meetings
Product Presentations
Concerts
Fairs
Trade Shows
Tours
Spouse Programs
Themed Galas

Hospitality Suites
Rallies
Fashion Shows
Community Events
Sales Events
Employee Holiday Events
Motivational Meetings
Press Conferences
Award Ceremonies

On the pages that follow, we will discuss the particular objectives and strategies for each of these events.

Themes

The following is a list of themes which could possibly be used for your special event:

Puttin' on the Ritz
The Halloween Haunt
Food-Flags-Fun of Many Countries
Tex-Mex Mix
A Carousel Celebration
Tara . . . A Burning Memory
The Classics in Concert
The "Lucille" Ball
Rock 'n Roll Revival
Mark Twain Lives On
"Can Can" Salute to Paris
The Color-The Drama-The Dream
The Nifty Gay Nineties
Fly Me to the Moon
The Beatles Beat Forever
One Giant Step . . . The Moon
T.V. Classics . . . Another Era
July Fourth Celebration . . . "The Big Boom"
Let Freedom Ring

Twelve Months of Merriment
Meeting the Challenge
Shoot Out at the O.K. Corral
"Splash!" . . . Everybody In!
Murder Mystery Mayhem
Call to the Post
The Gum Ball
Luke and Leah
Cafe Jazz
State Fair Frolic
Super Bowl Salute
The Orient Express Murder
Out of this World
Chinese New Year Celebration
Treasure Hunting for Toys
Key Stone Kops
New Year's Resolutions
Caribbean Carnival
Rodeo on Revue
A Golden Opportunity
Cinderella's Ball . . . The Slipper Fits!
A Kaleidoscopic Adventure
Big Band Bash
Mother Goose Madness
Halloween Hairytales
California Boys and Girls
Visionaries View of Fashion
The Wizard of Ozzie and Harriett
Western Round-Up
Going for the Gold
Baby Boomers Convention
Future Fantasia
Let's Go to the Hop
Mardi Gras
Platter Party
Showboat
Romance in Bloom

The Fabulous Fifties
The Big Apple
The Fantastic Forties
Elvis Lives On
At the Big Top
Casino Craze
Hooray for Hollywood
Pride in Presidents
Comedians of Our Time
Moonlight Hayride
Summer Camp
A Royal Affair
Masked Intrigue
M*A*S*H Bash
Plane Fun
The Snow Ball
International Ball
Roman Holiday
Gridiron Gallop
Spring Picnic
Movie Madness
Luau Aloha
A Desert Dash
Carnival in Rio
Santa's Christmas Fantasy
Flight Deck Party
Cruise Ship Shape-Up
A Not So Square Dance
Fred and Ginger
Funopoly
U.S.O. Show
Fractured Fairytales
Monkey Business
Winter Wonderland
Jubilation Jubilee
Alice in Wonderful Land
"Puff" the Magic Panther

Table 4 Budget Form

EXPENSES

Site
        Facility Rental
        Service Staff   _____
        Equipment Rental   _____
        Tables and Chairs   _____

Refreshments
        Food
        Alcohol   _____
        Linens   _____
        Rentals   _____
        Labor   _____
        Plus tax   _____

Invitations
        Artist/Photographer
        Printing   _____
        Postage   _____
        Processing   _____

Decorations
        Flowers
        Candles   _____
        Lighting   _____
        Balloons, etc.   _____
        Paper Supplies   _____
        Props   _____

Entertainment
        Travel, hotel, etc.   _____
        Lighting, staging   _____

Specialty items
        Ribbons, plaques   _____
        Gifts   _____

Miscellaneous
        Telephone
        Transportation   _____
        Photocopying   _____
        Postage   _____
        Facsimile service   _____

TOTAL   _____

Table 5 Talent Checklist

Talent's name_____

Phone number _____

Scheduled time of arrival _____

Scheduled time of departure _____ _____

Piano or musical accompaniment needed? _____

     Describe needs _____

Sound equipment necessary?_____

     Tape player_____   Speakers_____

microphones____stand____lavaliere_____ hand-held_____

Costumes — What do you provide?_____

          What do we provide? _____

Props — What do you bring?_____

          What do we bring?_____

(You must provide makeup, shoes, undergarments)

Dressing room space needed?_____(M)_____(F)_____

Description of job_____

_____

_____

Event objectives_____

_____

_____

Company's message_____

_____

Audience description_____

_____

Table 6 Catering Agreement

Caterer_____ Phone_____

Contact_____Facility_____# People____

Day and date of event_____Start_____Stop_____

Type of menu_____

_____

_____

_____

Days notice on final count_____

Price per person on menu $_____

Above price includes _____

_____

Rentals (tables, chairs, etc.) _____.

_____

_____

Caterer will arrive at: _____# Service people_____

Uniform specification_____

*Tables, chairs linens and set-up is the responsibility of the caterer.

*We understand the above prices are inclusive unless otherwise stated.

*The presentation of the food will be attractive and professional.

*Any suggestions for menu changes are welcome, but please inform prior to
  event.

* * *

It is the responsibility of the caterer to leave the facility clean— all garbage disposed of according to management specifications, break down and stacking of tables and chairs, ensuring floors are clean.

No solicitation will be allowed by any services hired during the event. This includes signage, busines cards or verbal communication.

(Your company)   Caterer

by:_____   by:_____

Chapter
4

The
Ground Breaking

CHAPTER 4

THE GROUNDBREAKING
Digging In to Produce a Dedication

A Groundbreaking is the ceremonial turning of the first piece of earth at the construction site of a building or other structure. It symbolizes the beginning of an exciting project for those who have been dreaming of and planning its existence for a long time.

The purpose of the groundbreaking is to promote the project being embarked upon, and to start selling the product or service that the new facility is being built to supply. An important additional benefit of such an event is to announce the coming of the building or other project to those who could be of assistance to the organization, whether financially, in cutting red tape, or through promotional word-of-mouth sales.

Since the groundbreaking represents the beginning of a project and not its completion, the primary audience for such an event is the press. A groundbreaking is often staged to get media attention, in hopes they will promote the project positively. This kind of advance publicity can prove invaluable to virtually any business or organization, which means you must make your groundbreaking newsworthy with some creative planning.

The following is a checklist to use in planning your groundbreaking:

— Check community and business calendars for conflicting dates
— Set the date for the event
— Invite dignitaries
— Gather an appropriate list of guests
— Update your media list

— Determine the event's desired image
— Create the overall concept
— Develop a theme
— Develop a budget
— Design and print the invitations
— Prepare the envelopes
— Mail invitations three weeks prior to event
— Print promotional materials to be given out at the event
— Print personalized items, such as name badges, napkins
— Procure a registration book
— Measure the event site
— Determine event signage
— Interview decorators
— Design the decor
— Determine sound and lighting needs
— Interview and select caterer
— Determine the menu
— Determine rental needs and source
— Determine mementos to be given out
— Hire all additional needed services
— Send contractual communications to hired services
— Interview management for press releases; write and send
— Communicate verbally with the press
— Confirm with all dignitaries in writing
— Confirm with all hired services in writing
— Prepare ceremony agenda according to protocol
— Prepare work schedule and staff assignments
— Manage all hired services and staff
— Decorate and make sure that all equipment is in place
— Check the sound system
— Greet the dignitaries
— Instruct management of positions and agenda
— Assemble guests for ceremony
— Disbursement of mementos
— Management of clean-up
— Pay bills
— Critique the event

Checklists are excellent tools to make certain that all of the most important details are covered. But while these lists will go a long way toward guaranteeing a successful event, the most important aspect of any groundbreaking is creativity. A unique, creative approach is vital to attract the attention of the media and to develop public loyalty to your organization through the event. You want to create a positive, memorable experience for your guests — a memory that down the road will trigger a desired action: either purchase of the product or service, or at least word-of-mouth promotion of the same. Like other special events, the groundbreaking serves as an indicator of the enthusiastic, first-class operation you are running.

To create such a positive memory, brainstorm with a group of other creative people who are knowledgeable about the project, to develop an effective overall concept. Strive for continuity of theme and concept throughout all of the printed pieces and visual elements that your guests will experience.

Your audience — especially the press — needs to believe that something new is going to happen at your groundbreaking ceremony. And to the extent that it is possible, don't disappoint them! Even traditional "shovels-in-the-dirt" groundbreakings can be embellished to make the event truly memorable and different.

The other critical consideration in planning your groundbreaking, or any special event for that matter, is determining the time that will be necessary to get everything accomplished during the event. Look at the many elements of the groundbreaking. Add the other things you feel are genuinely important to your purpose. Determine the number of hours that you feel the event will take to produce from concept to completion, then multiply that number by three. It is a realistic rule of thumb in this business that it always takes three times longer than anticipated to accomplish everything you want to get done. Since this might result in a marathon instead of a memorable event, you must consider very carefully those elements that will best promote your project in a positive and effective manner through this groundbreaking event.

CASE STUDY I

A major chemical company was moving into a rural but fast-developing community. The company wanted to become an integral and accepted part of the community. They wanted to get off to a good start by presenting a unique gift to the community, and they wanted to utilize as many local suppliers as possible. This meant working closely with and seeking advice from people in local government.

Answering the company's creative needs first, the following promotional concepts were proposed and initiated by my special events firm:

Theme — The community and its new corporate resident were tied together using the universal language of music, under the theme, "Let's Band Together." To this end, a song was produced and named for the city. A top country recording group, which happened to come from that community, was commissioned to write and record the song, which would then be performed as a world premiere at the groundbreaking, and each guest received a complimentary tape of the song. The song itself was given to the city as a gift from the company to be used to promote the town.

There was picnic-type food and entertainment at the event.

During the groundbreaking, an aerial photo was taken of the event and its guests. This photo was then used to create a commemorative poster to be given away several months later at the facility's grand opening.

A musically-themed billboard was erected in front of the building site and then periodically updated to inform the community of construction progress.

This "progress board" was photographed regularly and sent to local newspapers along with a press release, creating additional awareness of the new chemical plant in the community.

The theme for the grand opening, planned to occur one year after the groundbreaking, would be "Strike Up the Band" — a natural extension of the existing theme.

This musical concept was well received by the chemical company, and production began immediately on its various elements.

The first steps, as outlined in the pre-event checklist given earlier, included setting the date for the event by clearing it against local community and dignitary calendars, developing the budget, and determining the image and message to be projected. A logotype was developed for use on the invitation, napkins, mementos, name badges and balloons.

Site visits were used to determine the precise locations for all activities planned for the event as well as for the placement of electric lines, telephones, and tents. Interviews with local service vendors, including caterers and musicians, were conducted. Signage copy was written and the signs were ordered, along with flags and flagpoles (something to consider when you are trying to attract attention to any kind of new facility).

Because of the size of the anticipated crowd, portable toilets were secured and the local emergency medical service was alerted. The fire department agreed to be present during the event, and the police came out to assist with the parking and traffic control. (This illustrates the importance of early consultation with local government officals. Of course, when your organization is bringing jobs and tax revenues to a new location, you will find that the local authorities can be very cooperative.) Guards were hired to stay overnight with the tent and rental equipment, and a Color Guard was hired to give formality to the occasion.

Confirmation letters were mailed detailing the date, time, and place of the event to all the hired services as well as all dignitaries who were to take part in the ceremony. Press releases were sent to all local media and then followed up with telephone calls to help ensure adequate press coverage. Aggressive pursuit of this important goal resulted in an excellent turnout: five regional television stations sent crews, and every important local paper sent reporters and photographers. Special decor was developed to provide an interesting focal point for the cameramen.

Two live bands — including the "name" country group commissioned to record the theme song — were hired to enliven the event.

Although many items had been delivered and facilities set up the previous day, the event management team arrived at 7 a.m., three hours before the scheduled start of the groundbreaking ceremony. Using a prepared day-of-the-event agenda, each service vendor was checked off upon arrival. The official photographer was given a list of specific pictures to be taken, and company managers and local dignitaries were pointed out to him as they arrived.

Just before 10 a.m., the first band began to play for arriving guests. Members of the event staff greeted dignitaries, gave them event agendas and press releases, and introduced them to company managers. Representatives of the press were also greeted with news releases and agendas, and introduced to the company's management in order to be interviewed for news stories.

An experienced master of ceremonies had been hired to lend a more professional image to the event (although in many cases it can prove difficult to dissuade management from having one of their own perform this demanding role). At the appointed hour, the emcee cued the various groups involved that the ceremony was about to begin and invited the dignitaries to take their predetermined and marked places on stage.

The ceremony began with an invocation delivered by a local minister (religious leaders should always be included on your list of dignitaries), followed by the necessary speeches. Then the dignitaries, including the governor, city and local officials, and representatives of the company were asked to step down from the stage and help "break ground."

As the final shovelful of dirt was turned, the band broke into their world premiere of the company's unique gift to the community: its very own song. Not only did the performance receive a standing ovation, but a few tears of emotion and pride were seen as well.

The ceremony was closed with a benediction, and the audience was asked to assemble in the predesignated area for official photographs, including the aerial shot mentioned previously. Refreshments and entertainment followed, and professionally-produced tapes of the community song were distributed to every guest.

After the guests departed, each service vendor cleaned up his area, packed equipment and left. Our event team policed the site for trash and any equipment that might have been left behind. The rental company arrived to remove the tents and other rental items. All that remained to be done was to approve invoices and pay bills — and, of course, to hold a critiquing session to evaluate the event's success and determine new and better ways to manage the next one.

Outdoor events lend themselves to blockbuster presentations! These 50-foot air tubes highlighted a major chemical company's ground breaking and introduction to the community.

This groundbreaking was exciting, fun, and, most of all, highly successful. Every invited state, county, and local dignitary was present, and general attendance was quite large as well.

The community song was the biggest success of all. It captured perfectly the flavor and attitude of the area, and not surprisingly became a local radio favorite.

The special decor mentioned earlier consisted of enormous, 50-foot-long helium balloons, anchored to the ground in clusters of red, blue, green, yellow, and white. Considering the event site consisted of a large empty lot, these were perfect for both breaking up the space and for creating visual interest. They also provided a unique and colorful focal point for the television and newspaper photographers. Most important, they were memorable and helped to create an indelible impression on everyone in attendance.

An important aspect of this event was adapting it to the many subtle, but significant differences in this small, rural community's tastes and habits. There is no single right or wrong way to handle any such event — but there probably is a best way to make this or any other particular audience feel comfortable. Operating in a setting or a culture different than what you're accustomed to requires a sensitivity to the needs and concerns of others. You can suggest that things might be better handled your way, but keep your mind open to doing things their way — with a few of your own improvements. If the local caterer tells you that people there like their hamburgers served with sauerkraut, then give him the benefit of the doubt. The whole point of a groundbreaking, after all, is to introduce the company as a friendly new neighbor. Anything that helps you achieve that purpose should be accepted gracefully and gratefully.

Chapter
5

The
Grand Opening

CHAPTER 5

THE GRAND OPENING
Organizing a Celebratory Commencement

A great Grand Opening is like a swat on the baby's (company's!) bottom to get it to breathe! You need to shout to your potential customers that you are there and ready to be a part of their world. A business can exist for months, even years, before enough people notice it to make the necessary business difference.

In addition, a grand opening is a unique marketing tool. Seldom will you ever have the opportunity for media attention as you will when you are opening a new business or facility. By its very definition, it is a *special* event that cannot happen again, so make it

Festive balloons, dignitaries, ribbons and large scissors are traditional elements in a grand opening ceremony.

memorable. It tells the business community that the company is ready to contribute to the economy, communicates that you are a winner, and brings customers to the door.

When the opportunity is there to make a business turn a profit better and faster — go for it!

As in other special event projects, it is imperative to begin all work with the basic information that comes from "creative brainstorming": overall concept, theme, decor, graphic consistency, etc.

From there, a list such as the following can be developed:

— Send the designed invitations out for bids

— Determine cost of facility rental

— Select 3 candidates for catering and get bids

— Determine rental needs and costs

— Need a tent? Will it need lighting, flooring, heating, or air conditioning?

— The many elements of decorating need to be broken down and priced

— Professional services must be determined

— Communication systems need to be evaluated

— Transportation needs to be assessed

— Is there a need for ticket sales? How will this be done?

— Signage needs are to be determined

— Is a hospitality suite needed?

— Are specialty give-away items needed?

— Awards are to be determined and engraved

— Printing needs: napkins, stationary, labels, etc.

— Guest register should be procured

— Name badges purchased/printed, written and filed for easy disbursement

— Florists will be hired by determination of their capabilities, equipment and prices

— Entertainment needs are to be researched and hired

— Theatrical needs — staging, backdrops, props?

— Lighting for different areas is to be evaluated

— Sound evaluation is necessary

— Photographer should be hired

— Limousines, if needed, are to be ordered

— Determine needs and costs of videotaping event

— Tickets for events are to be purchased

— Hotel accommodations need to be researched and made

— Considerations for special guests, retirees and spouses?

— Acquire gifts for supporters, speakers, etc.

— Promotional costs should be estimated according to an outline of needs

— Labor needs and costs should be determined

— Accounting system needs to be developed

— Is your insurance coverage adequate?

— Are your mailing lists updated and accurate?

— Determine auxiliary events and break them down for planning

— Negotiate, sign, and return contracts between all necessary parties

— Put event on community/convention calendar if appropriate

— Be aware of any events conflicting with your event

— Reassess your food and catering plans

— Plan a rehearsal

— Devise a budget for last minute expenses

— Are water and electrical supplies adequate?

— Determine an area from which to manage the event on site

— Prepare a rain plan or a rain date

— Prepare a time schedule for organization of the event

— Prepare a work/time schedule for the day of the event

— Prepare a time schedule (agenda) for the event itself

— Assign event responsibilities, including shifts if necessary

— Will you need meals for the staff the day of the event?

— Has anything been forgotten?

A balloon sculpture of the company's logo dominated the background for a ceremonial grand opening. The specially-designed 40-foot "ribbon" triggered an exciting balloon release when cut. The event theme was appropriately named "Molecular Momentum."

CASE STUDY II

A swimming pool company wanted to thank friends, contractors, and employees for getting them to the point of "opening the doors" of a new facility.

A date for the event was determined based on the maximum attendance potential of their audience and the areas' dignitaries.

A budget was developed to accomplish the primary goal; to project a quality, first-class image for the company.

The invitation list was completed. Suggestions for guests came from everyone in sales, service, and management. The Board of Directors also contributed names they felt were important.

An invitation was designed and printed that made a statement of quality, and suggested that something "special" would happen at the event. This included a whimsical graphic of a family of four, swimming to the event. These animated people were later used on the permanent sign on the front of the building.

People were hired to hand-write, stuff, and stamp the invitations.

The warm water, romantic implications of the company's products, swimming pools and spas, lead our creative team naturally to a tropical theme, which included a Polynesian menu and drinks, and the hiring of an appropriate caterer. Orchids were flown in from Hawaii to float in a pool that had a fountain in the center. The orchids lent their color to other tropical plants and some were also assembled to become the 30-foot "ribbon" for the ceremonial cutting.

Signage was prepared to direct people from the surrounding streets to the front door. Uniformed security police were hired to park cars and set an early professional attitude about the event.

Name badges with the "family of four" logo were filled out and worn by all attendees, who also signed the guest register. These names were used by the company's sales people for follow-up calls. The staff wore plastic badges with the event logo as well as their name and title. Napkins were also printed with this logo.

Hawaiian orchids were extravagantly designed to form a unique ribbon. The "ribbon cutting" was part of the grand opening ceremony and dedication for a swimming pool company.

There was informational signage at all strategic areas. The facility was continually monitored throughout the event for neatness.

A musical group provided pleasing background music for informal conversation.

The facility had been visually readied for tours, and the guests arrived to warm greetings from the staff and management. The atmosphere was professional, and the projected image was first class: all of the objectives had been met. The company was ready to move on to the next phase of their opening.

Management was interviewed to develop the correct message for a press release for the media. A press release was written and sent to the local business editors.

Dignitaries of the state, county, city, and local districts were invited to attend and participate in the event.

An agenda was developed, according to ceremonial protocol, to include these dignitaries and accomplish the many "thank you" messages that were to be extended at this event.

Phase Two was the general public grand opening. This included newspaper advertisements with the "family of four" logo and enticing specials on swimming pools and spas. Television advertising was included.

The public grand opening included signage and colorful balloons inside, outside and on top of the building. Hot dogs and soft drinks were another part of the enticement, as were the mascots of the local college sports teams.

A booth at a home show was also used as a source of promoting the new facility. Invitations were printed and distributed to people interested in attending a "Spa Party," an open house to which they wore swimsuits in order to "try before you buy" a spa. This was the owner's idea, and proved to be a very good marketing tool.

In addition, a newsletter was created and distributed at the show and handed out for the first few weeks of operation, discussing the new facility and facts on warm water recreation.

Shortly after these events, the company invited a segment of their clientele into the new facility for all-day educational seminars and lunch. This included an exciting promotional invitation, spouse entertainment, the necessary set-up and speakers. In addition, sponsors were solicited for prizes which were given away after the meetings.

These events have proven to be successful with the passing of time. This company continues to enjoy sales far ahead of projections.

A note on this grand opening: We had worked fast and hard all day, and had completed decorating about an hour and a half before the event. At that time, I invited the client to examine and discuss the overall look of his showroom. He said that he had expected more color. We all had had a mental picture of Hawaiian flowers producing a lush array of tropical color, and had obviously transferred that image in our conversations. Being extremely sensitive to pleasing the client, I sent out for more flowers — more flowers, colorful flowers — one hour before the event. They truly made the difference. We were all pleased with their brilliant enhancement.

The point is that the Hawaiian flowers sounded fabulous, but they were not as large or as colorful as we had imagined. Our "vision" was not realistic.

This has happened several times — an event has been decorated and we stand back with the decorator for a final critique before he packs up his equipment and leaves. We have a sense of "This doesn't look the way I thought it would." We have tried to avoid this empty feeling of "what can we do now" by drawing our expectations on paper, asking the decorators to show us more detail in their drawings, thorough discussions at the beginning, and allowing more time for another approach.

Whenever possible, we request samples of proposed floral arrangements, or go to prop warehouses to see backdrops or other equipment. Photographs of the decorator's previous jobs where similar elements have been used can help one visualize how they will look in your situation. Photographs will also tell you how that vendor works and their overall results.

It also helps to develop a rapport with one decorator. He will begin to understand the way you think. In our case, our favorite decorator now knows to add a good dose of flamboyance and flair to his original thoughts; so do our florists, our sign painters, our caterers and so on.

CASE STUDY III

A newly completed, eleven acre manufacturing facility, that employed 500 people, needed to be acknowledged with a special celebration.

Planning began seven months in advance for this project. A Sunday-through-Tuesday time frame was selected by the committee as appropriate for the goals to be accomplished. Calendars of dignitaries were cleared, as well as industry related dates, since many in the audience were distributors of the company's products. Employees and their families were also of primary importance on the guest list.

A futuristic concept was created. The theme cleverly included the product and company's message, "Building For Tomorrow — It's Right Around the Cabinet!" The graphics were futuristic. Silver foil on white chrome stock was used for folders, name badges, and invitations. Stationery and envelopes were printed to give continuity, and to help promote the theme before and after the event. Banners for parking attendants, tour guides and registration people were printed using the logo. Balloons with the logo were put in with employee's paychecks as promotions of attendance. White napkins with silver foil were ordered, as well as pencils, scratch pads, and other special mementos. Futuristic silver costumes and wigs were ordered for the catering staff.

A state-of-the-art tent, 145 feet by 120 feet, was erected at the site —on the new asphalt parking lot. Holes, which were later filled, were drilled to ensure the tent's security. This point needs to be considered when combining the use of a tent with a new structure which will also have a new asphalt parking lot.

This tent was used on Sunday to provide a festive area for entertainment, refreshments, and shade from the sun. On Monday, it was transformed into a nightclub for a sit-down dinner and stage show, where a futuristic atmosphere was created with the use of decorator elements such as mylar and neon lights.

Golf carts and walkie-talkies were rented for the Sunday Grand Opening, due to the size of the property and the need to communicate quickly. Portable restrooms were rented and discreetly camouflaged with tents. Emergency medical units were on location because of the size of the facility, crowd (estimated at 3,000), and the heat of the day. Police were alerted of possible congestion; they established an effective flow of traffic at the street entrance.

All of these items — and more — were a part of an approved budget. Through "give and take" in the many areas of expenditures, this budget was within 4% of the original figure.

Site visits with the vendors were necessary for determining the tour route, staging, signage, caterer location, parking requirements, lighting, sound, work areas, and tent location.

Meetings with management and employee committees were frequent in order to keep them aware of progress and listen to their desires and concerns.

Contracts were developed and sent to all of the services selected for the events.

The airport was notified as to the time and location of the ceremonial balloon release.

Hotel accommodations, including food and meeting rooms, and all ground transportation were arranged for the distributors who came in for the occasion.

The Regional Airport Authority also gave us permission to set up a "Welcome" area in the terminal to greet our incoming guests.

A tour map with the logo was printed, which included photographs of the manufacturing equipment, and descriptive copy, to give to guests for a greater understanding of the tour and product assembly.

Labor projections and time schedules were developed for the week, the day before, and the day of the event. Equipment receiving and pick-up schedules were developed and sent to the many people involved.

Sunday, Open House/Grand Opening day, started at 4:00 a.m. Arrangements had to be made to enable entrance into certain areas of the plant to begin preparations. The balloon company arrived first. It took many hours to inflate the thousands of balloons used to decorate the facility and fill the nets for the final balloon release. Helium balloons were also filled to be given out to all of the children.

Hundreds of stanchions and miles of ribbon were used along

the eleven-acre tour. The setting up and removal of these stanchions required major amounts of time, equipment and labor.

The receiving and setting up of goods and props had been going on all week. Positioning the many elements — lights, sound, food service equipment, tents, signage, parking barricades and staging — required a fast pace and an energetic crew.

Oversized replicas of the company's best-selling cabinet door, 16 feet by 16 feet, were erected on the stage, at the entrance to the facility. During the ceremony, dignitaries and company management exchanged well wishes. The finale of fanfares from a brass ensemble noted the rising of pre-arranged futuristic vapor coming from beneath the large cabinet doors. As the doors dramatically rumbled open,

The stage was set for excitement with these giant replicas of cabinet doors that served as the backdrop for a cabinet company's grand opening celebration.

thousands of colorful balloons flew into the beautiful afternoon sky. The crowd applauded enthusiastically, and as invited, came up on the stage, passed through the doors and began traveling the Path of Pride — the beginning of the tour. The "path" was designed with periodic "Burma Shave" type signs reading "Pride in People — Pride in Product — Pride in Productivity," etc. This was developed to involve and educate the guests about the company's mission and the event's

The giant doors rumbled open, smoke bellowed out and a brilliant balloon release invited the guests into the facility for informative tours.

message.

The machinery was designed to come alive with a variety of exciting lighting effects. As mentioned earlier, each strategic point included signage, balloons, and a tour guide to provide information. Each point was also marked on the brochure.

A large cake, designed to resemble the new facility, was on display in the tent. Fun foods like hot dogs, popcorn, soft drinks and ice cream were served from vending carts on the grounds. Balloons were given to the children by "futuristic clowns."

The clean-up of such an event was thoroughly planned. The removal of the many stanchions and ribbons was a major effort, as it took two hours, four golf carts, two trailers, and 16 people working intensely to get the stanchions out of the way so that work could begin on Monday morning.

All of the rented equipment had to be put in one area for pick up to avoid both an additional day's charge, and any confusion.

The parking lot was necessarily cleaned.

The employees' pride was renewed as they took their families through their work-place and explained their part in the overall operation.

Day two for the distributors — a full day of meetings, including a new product unveiling — was scheduled for Monday. The futuristic approach of silver costumes, smoke and colored revolving lights was used to dramatize the product, excite the distributors, and encourage sales. This continuity gave credibility to the theme and overall promotion.

Monday evening brought the 400 distributors back to the facility on buses for a celebration. Cocktails, hors d'oeuvres and musical entertainment were followed by a sit-down dinner. A live stage production was performed, based on the 50-year history of the company. This production generated an emotional high that sent these important company representatives back into the field with new pride and a renewed motivation to sell more of the company's product.

When the event was over, the billing reconciliation began. The many invoices needed approval according to contracts and agreements. Payments had to be made quickly, since many vendors worked on a cash basis.

This will always be one of my most memorable series of events. My sister came to visit that week to see what the event business was all about. I'm not sure if it was the number of people we handled, the number of events executed over a three day period, the thousands of balloons we positioned in this eleven-acre plant, or maybe the 98° weather when we were outside working in a tent for fourteen straight hours... but she doesn't ask about the business very much anymore, nor has she ever returned!

CASE STUDY IV

A highly respected printing company faced a unique problem that required a creative approach. The location of its new printing plant, and thus its grand opening, was 35 miles from their customer base. How were they going to get those important people to drive out to the event, after work, on a hot summer day?

A creative brainstorming session in our office produced a concept — "The Big Event" — that worked. "The Big Event" was proclaimed as being the biggest and best event of the year. "Oversized" elements were made — the invitation, registration book and pen, balloons for the plant tour and signage were all super-sized.

Large flowers were made out of the company's printed product, promotional newspaper inserts, and used in a huge centerpiece for the over-sized buffet table.

A *large* selection of *big* gifts were given away in a drawing.

The biggest contribution to success, however, was the ribbon that was cut following the formal ceremony. It was over 200 feet in length, four feet

"THE BIG EVENT" was so themed to excite and increase guest attendance at a very busy time and distant location. The BIG tent, BIG prizes and other BIG elements helped to carry out the message of this company's BIG capabilities.

in width, and stretched from one end of the new building to the other. Every customer had his own portion of the ribbon on which his name and logo were printed. They were given scissors and asked to stand by their section, and at the appropriate time, to assist with the ceremonial cutting. This ensured that a representative of each client was in attendance, thus accomplishing their main goal! The preparations for this event followed the same format as the other two grand openings; date determination, creative concept, press releases, site visits, and so on, up through the execution and bill paying. This was a good example of the need for, and the results of, effective creative brainstorming.

CASE STUDY V

The Regional Airport Authority challenged our firm, Master of Ceremonies, to create a state-of-the-art dedication of their beautiful new airside terminal. They wanted to create a historical documentation of the culmination of this major project. In addition, they wanted to celebrate their achievement and create a "send-off" that would produce publicity directed toward the airlines, board of directors, city and state dignitaries and business executives.

With these definite goals, and our audiences determined, we sat down to some heavy creative brainstorming. Our job was to reach beyond today, beyond our experiences and far beyond our local resources.

"Soaring On the Wings Of Progress" was the theme we created based on the Regional Airport Authority's's logo identity of a pegasus, their accomplishments and their attitudes.

The invitation was unlike any this audience had seen! A pegasus hologram gave continual movement to the highly-glossed black cover. A border of gold foil outlined the heavy oblong invitation with the theme produced in beautiful script, also in gold foil.

All the sights and sounds enjoyed by the more than 300 attendees were state-of-the-art.

The sounds included a specially produced soundscape, the sounds of airplanes taking off and landing, which welcomed guests and created the feeling of the surroundings. A pianist played up-beat classics at a grand piano close to the entrance and a full orchestra was positioned on the mezzanine to play fine music throughout the evening. In addition, we had regional music played by live combos at the ends of every concourse, to draw our visitors down for further inspection of the facility.

The sights began immediately with chaser lights on the handrails of the moving 300-foot sidewalk, creating futuristic excitement. The building had a rotunda, and a 32-foot dome, with concourses projecting like axles from a wheel hub. This room demanded a strong statement in the huge center. This is where we put our focal point. We created a "wish list" for our decorator of the possible elements to be included, to produce the overall image we wanted to project through this decor piece. He went beyond our desires! A 28-foot copper sculpture resembling a tree was created and placed in the center of a circular moving stage. On the branches of the sculpture were every yellow flower grown! Hand blown glass neon flowers were added to illuminate it when the day turned to dark, dramatically changing the appearance of the sculpture.

Eight-foot clear plexiglass tubes held bubbling water and swimming goldfish. Lava rocks, huge leaves and additional greenery supported the base of the sculpture.

Hors d'oeuvre tables were built to surround this 18-foot stage,

Focal point scale is extremely important in designing for a special event. Observe the height of the unique floral-covered copper sculpture and the circumference of the buffet table that mimics the domed ceiling's height and diameter. (Photography courtesy of Joe Edens Photography)

which added to the overall size of the focal point. Slate blue tables complemented the interior decor of the facility. The food was elegantly presented and accentuated with more yellow flowers and large leaves. (See the photo section for visual.) Four 12-foot copper glitter pillars were built into the tables, giving a regal look to the total picture.

Slate blue and glimmering copper lamé linens covered the gathering tables (a taller cocktail table).

The lighting was professionally set to subliminally enhance the many elements of decor, yet the equipment was well hidden in the dome by our experienced technicians.

The serving staff of forty, sporting new black and white tuxedo uniforms, served exceptional food and drink throughout the evening, including champagne for the ceremonial toast.

Many dignitaries attended and participated in saluting the new wing. As the copper lamé cover was removed from the dedication plaque, the promise of a Grand Finale exploded. Silver sparkling rockets shot up from the center of the huge focal point, across the room, totally encircling the rotunda exterior and spilled over the glass dome, high above everyone's heads! This spectacle was in concert to powerful futuristic music and hundreds of azure beams of laser lights.

The lasers shot up and down the corridors! The images landed on a specially-built screen where a custom-designed laser show, which told the story of the building of the terminal, dazzled the audience.

The guests were awed by their evening and carried away a memento to recreate the magic — a clear, lucite cube, that when turned a certain way, created a flying pegasus. This curosity was produced by a special laser process.

We were all very proud of our successful results, the Regional Airport Authority, our entire firm, and our many talented vendors, drawn from all around the United States to support this elaborate effort. These professionals, the decorators, the laser company, the lighting company and the pyrotechnics firm, were known to us through our affiliation with the International Special Events Society.

This event was created, organized and implemented in approximately ten weeks, which is miraculous! But, it *can* be done if you approach every detail systematically, creatively and professionally, using the guidelines stated in these pages.

Chapter
6

The
Open House

CHAPTER 6

THE OPEN HOUSE
An Invitation to Get Better Acquainted

The motivational factors for holding an Open House are to:

— Give your customers, members, peers, or the public in general, a first-hand look at your facility, your products, and the way you do business
— Introduce a new service or product
— Show employees' families the work place
— Obtain media exposure

The desired goals are to:

— Develop loyalty
— Demonstrate your procedures
— Persuade your audience to your way of thinking
— Increase membership
— Improve sales
— Increase productivity

The methods of producing an open house are basically the same as outlined for the ground breaking and grand opening. *Using those guidelines* and your creatively designed concept, you can find success in fufilling your goals. The case study that follows will contain good examples to apply to your open house.

CASE STUDY VI

The 25th anniversary celebration of a packaging company was themed "25 Years of Boxing At Its Best." A silver boxing glove was used as the logo graphic, with "25" printed inside the outline of the glove.

This graphic was used on a very cleverly designed invitation, a pop-open card. The printing was done in-house by the client, which is always effective because it is proof of their quality capabilities.

A new and very state-of-the-art computerized printing press was also to be introduced at this event, so our goals were two-fold. A special poster would be printed on the new press that evening to be given to guests as a commemorative memento.

This packaging company's milestone anniversary event successfully informed and entertained its targeted audience through the theme, "25 Years of Boxing at Its Best." Guided tours reminded guests of the company's quarter century of commitment to customer service and quality.

As guests entered the facility, they were greeted by a friendly staff serving as tour guides and good-will ambassadors. They visited the newly decorated offices, and then went into the plant for tours.

The machines were in operation, so the guests could get a good idea of the procedures and capabilities. The tour route was lined with blue carpet, the corporate color, as well as stanchions and ribbons. At the areas of special interest, a large sign had been painted describing the particular press function. Attention was brought to the signs with large bouquets of blue, silver and hot pink balloons, along with oversized boxing glove cut-outs with numbers in the center. These numbers coordinated with numbers printed in a handout describing

CHAPTER 7

CONVENTIONS
Creating an Effective Assembly

Conventions are an important part of the life of corporations and associations. There are four basic, equally important elements of a convention: business and educational meetings, networking, motivation, and, rest and relaxation. Obviously, the business meeting provides the opportunity to discuss information that is pertinent to the industry and to make decisions about the organization. Seminars, speakers, panel discussions, and trade shows are the educational component. Networking allows participants to discuss with peers the issues that are pertinent to their particular industry. The information that is shared can prove to be invaluable. Motivation to produce an ongoing positive attitude about your organization or project is essential to your growth. Rest and relaxation are also a productive part of the participants' time spent at a convention. Often meetings are intense; something fun to do to unwind is advantageous to the overall goals.

The first consideration when organizing a convention is timing. It will take at least one year to plan. It can be done in six months, but it is not advisable, especially if the event is to be a big one. Time is your ally, and a shortage of time can be a real problem.

After choosing several alternate times, do some research to find out what other events might be planned locally or nationally that could possibly conflict with your plans, thereby causing poor attendance.

With one or two dates in mind, a decision on a city and a facility can be made. The location of the corporate headquarters may be a deciding factor. It is advantageous for participants to be able to take plant tours and to meet people they talk with every day on the telephone. Or, if attendance needs improving, a resort site would be a good alternative. At this point, it would be helpful to engage a professional meeting planner who knows which places would be appropriate.

Negotiations will begin with the chosen location. The company's requirements must be made perfectly clear at the start. Prices must be complete in order to have a clear understanding of value for costs. All aspects must be considered very carefully — parking, other conventions being held at the same facility, tipping, free van service or any hidden costs. Billing procedures need to be clearly outlined and understood, with authorized signatures on file. Financial responsibility should be reviewed, and a decision made (with participants being made aware of what they may or may not charge) on the master account. If there are changes during the planning of the event, notify the facility immediately, so they can be prepared, and so there will be no question about billing later. A contract will be drafted and signed, and the company is obliged to abide by it even if there was a misunderstanding. Corporations usually give the contract to their lawyers for approval before signing. The facility will send the company a final bill after all charges are collected and computed. The invoice must be examined carefully and compared to the contract before payment is made.

Once the time, date, and location are firm, goals must be determined and the message established. If it is exciting enough, sometimes the name of the city can be incorporated into the theme. The more exciting the theme and concept, the greater the attendance is likely to be. Think new and big thoughts!

Having made the other important decisions, the budget now needs to be established. It will include a list of anticipated expenditures balanced against revenues or the allowance from the corporate budget. The registration fee is the largest portion of the revenue, unless there is income from exhibitors at a trade show. Sponsors may contribute if they are offered enough exposure to the right buying group. If the revenue from a combination of sponsors, registration fees, and booths is $180,000 for a convention of 500 people for three days, obviously expenses should stay within that amount. Once the budget is approved, the management team will use it as their bible.

A working calendar with what needs to be done and when, must be developed. This should be as sacred as the budget.

Whether this is the first year for the convention or the 25th, the company must promote the event. Maximizing the attendance will give a greater return on investment of time and money. The more people who respond, the more information there is to be shared. A large turnout will also make a positive impression on the participants. Be thorough with the promotions. Communicate all the anticipated questions of the recipients very clearly and concisely. What do the participants want to hear about this convention? What will convince them to attend? The materials used in the printed matter is important. An expert printer, a good graphic designer, and clever copy writer are paramount to producing professional and creative promotional material. The use of color can be effective, especially if there are certain colors associated with the corporate logo. Quality can mean different things to different groups. Try to imagine what the person receiving the information would like to see. Developing a timetable for the printed work is next. It should be established by working backwards from the date the guests are to actually receive the invitation. Allow at least two weeks for printing uncomplicated jobs and one to two weeks for stuffing envelopes, addressing and stamping envelopes (take into account the size of the mailing list and the work force available to complete the in-house portion of the mailing). Often the registration form is attached to the promotional piece. It should be simple. If the reader feels that it is too complicated, he will put off filling it out and unconsciously have a negative attitude about the convention as a whole.

Promotional materials sent to the particpants should include:

— Date, time, place
— A full agenda of the meeting
— Suggestions for dress for each of the events
— Activities that are scheduled for leisure time
— Confirmed travel arrangements including:
  flight arrangements, hotel accommodations,
  shuttle service, taxi or bus information,
  maps and lists of local attractions
— A clear picture of what is expected during the meeting
— Who is attending

As the date of the convention draws near and all the planning has been completed, the last item to consider is how to guarantee smooth sailing for the actual event. The best way to accomplish this is to meet with as many vendors as possible and with the hotel staff to go over every detail of the next few days activities. Point out the coordinators by name and make sure that each person knows who owns what responsibility — a written list is very helpful. A good attitude and a smiling face go a long way to making a fun, successful convention.

Over a period of years, a scheduling pattern for corporate conventions has emerged as follows:

Registration — This sets the tone for the whole convention. If it is smooth and the convention staff has been well informed, all should go well. Lines, confusion, irritable personnel, missing papers or information, names misspelled, incorrect promotional material, special needs not met, incomplete registration packets will all create bad tempers. On the other hand, if there are happy faces (people who seem genuinely glad to be hosting a convention), balloons, or other festive preparations, the participants will anticipate a great event.

A "greeting" event — This is usually a cocktail or hors d'oeuvres party. Name tags are given and business cards exchanged while networking.

Opening day welcome — A greeting is traditionally extended at the beginning of the first full day of the meeting. The organization leader often addresses the group and thanks them for coming.

Meetings and seminars — Normally, sessions will last for about three hours with a break of fifteen minutes or one-half hour in between. The information given during these meetings is the reason for the convention, so it must be presented in a thoroughly polished manner or possibly using professional speakers. A speakers bureau is a good source for nationally-known personalities. They can be special interest or motivational speakers. If someone of that calibre is retained, expect a big portion of the budget to go to their fee. A nationally-known speaker will charge an average of $10,000 plus accommodations. A regionally known celebrity will cost about $3,000, and a local speaker will be in the range of $1,000. For a local or regional personality, the Yellow Pages or local chapter of the Speakers Bureau are the best sources. Take advantage of speakers' videos or tapes to make your hiring decision; they are helpful tools. Lunches can also be an educational time if you have a keynote speaker.

A trade-show or exhibit is a "win-win" situation for everyone. Exhibitors have the opportunity to display their products or services to a carefully selected audience. And through entrance fees and booth rentals their presence assists with the expenses of the convention. The participants are exposed to state-of-the-art products and can obtain detailed information directly from the representative of the company that produces the item. Often purchases are made at the "show" at discount prices.

As the convention continues, the level of excitement must be maintained. This can be accomplished by "programming" the participants with the idea that they are having a wonderful time and will want to come back again next year. Friendly, courteous service from the management team is a good example. This kind of hospitality can determine the success or failure of an event. This is done in small, often unconscious ways, such as positive captions on note paper or an enthusiastic emcee at the podium.

The finale should be power-packed. The messages, "We are glad you came," "Remember the good times we had" and "Come back next year" are all important to impress upon the participants. The evening should be designed to fit the particular group attending. It could be a dinner dance or a banquet with awards and a speaker or a gala, if the budget can handle it. The gala has my vote! A cocktail party, followed by a wonderful meal in a splendidly decorated ball-room of an elegant hotel or grand mansion is an impressive way to say that a company will go to every possible means to please its guests. The finale is an investment with a guaranteed return. In addition, the host organization will appreciate it after they have worked so hard to make the event pleasurable for everyone else.

The final session is the last chance to impart information, so make it meaningful. It would also be a good time to pass out a questionnaire that would allow the participants to evaluate their experience. If possible, structure your approach with a positive slant (a technique that is used at Disney World), so that the person filling it out will have a more positive attitude about their experience.

Carefully review these results in a meeting with all of the

original planning committee. Have both a tape recorder and a stenographer present at the meeting, as well as appropriate vendors. Discuss the positives and the negatives. Discuss the facility, date, time, registration statistics, attendance at each event, hotel accomodations, trade exhibitions, entertainment for spouses and families, and budget. The reason for doing this is to make plans for next year.

When saying goodbye, present the date and location for next year's event. People will be impressed with the "look-ahead" approach of the company, and they will be programmed to anticipate the next convention.

Iridescent foliage, magnificent florals and high-tech plexiglass tubes sporting goldfish is a decorator's dream. A descriptive wish list of elements provided to the decorator produced outstanding results at this Grand Opening. (Photograph courtesy of Jay Ellis, Tent & Event Company, Bloomington, Indiana)

Wrapped in a golden bow, the Grand Opening for this health care administration office visually promised new opportunities.

Excitement and awe were produced at this event through pyrotechnics and a version of the event logo rendered in 450 five-inch mylar balloons. This revolving focal point of a trade show reflected a series of colorful lights to emphasize the theme, "Discover The Spectrum Of The Link." (Photograph courtesy of Richard Bramm)

A decorated carousel horse welcomed U.S. Senators to a private Derby celebration aptly themed "A Carouselabration." This unique Americana treasure was found in an antique store.

This bath house decor represented a miniature carousel, utilizing pastel balloons entwined with tiny clear lights secured to white carousel horses.

Peach, teal and pearl colors, along with the carousel theme, were used in the carriage house/dining area. The table decor followed the continuity with creatively-designed center-pieces. (Photographs courtesy of Richard Bramm)

Painted backdrops and imaginative props enthused guests at this western-themed event, the "Gold Rush Gala." (Photographs courtesy of Richard Bramm)

The theme "The Big Top" creatively reminded employees attending a sales meeting, that continued peak performance is necessary for lasting success.

WOW! Fascinating decor, a life-size carousel, a carnival of game tents, and a full-scale three-ring circus created a positive, "I want to come back next year" attitude for this convention finale.

Vividly clad clowns briefly took a back seat to watch the guests' performances.

Celebrations and festivals, such as the Kentucky Derby in Louisville, Kentucky, can mean rolling out the red carpet, along with southern hospitality and events galore.

Holidays can evoke extravagantly lavish settings. A musically themed dessert table entertained as well as tempted guests. An elaborate harpsichord, Victorian embellished mannequins, and festive florals created an exceptional centerpiece.

CASE STUDY VII

This convention was the second annual meeting of an industrial group that was attempting to form an association. Attracting participants was the first job, so a facility was chosen for its intimate atmosphere and beautiful setting. The goal was to have the largest crowd possible in order to have the greatest chance of signing up new members in the association. The theme was developed around the goal of selling memberships. The slogan was put on signs, badges, pencils, pads, and other promotional material. Industrial colors were chosen that were festive and product oriented. A good portion of the budget went into promotional pieces. Although the company was unable to spend a great deal of money, the overall impression of the event did not suffer because our professional coordinators were extremely organized and creative.

Registration was easy with this small group. The participants were greeted by smiling faces and well-planned packets which included their badges. The packets were arranged alphabetically, so there was no waiting in line. One person was seated at a separate table with information about local sites and restaurants.

A welcome cocktail reception was held in a section of the hotel's lovely ballroom, where we set up a trade show of 15 exhibitors. Participants mingled and got to know one another while looking at the various exhibits. The decorations consisted of glittered letters cut out and hung against a colorfully draped backdrop with balloons and columns on either side. Dinner was served, and afterward a motivational speaker was featured. The flowers that were used on the dinner tables were reused the next day at breakfast and lunch, with minor changes such as balloons and industry paraphernalia (one way of operating on a small budget).

The topics for the next day's meeting were sales and marketing, industry/association growth and success, and personnel management. There were coffee breaks in between and a delicious lunch in the middle of the day. Dinner was in a cheerful, sunny room in the lower level of the hotel. The dinner speaker was personable, with a topic of individual company growth.

A brunch was held on the last day in still another part of the hotel (moving about is a good way to interest people). Finally a short meeting was held to project an enthusiastic image of the organization, enlist memberships and say goodbye.

The convention was a great success. Initially, 100 people, including spouses, were expected and 138 registered. The membership drive was successful! Today that association enjoys great strength with a very large number of members. We like to think this is, in part, due to their initial effort and professionalism during this informative convention.

Table 7 Convention Registration Responsibilities

Convention Registration Responsibilities Check List

Job	Time Prior to Event
Recruit staff or volunteers. Determine price categories. Set deadlines for advance registration. Design registration form and promotion package.	12 months
Draw registration area diagram. Make policy decisions. Determine type of name tags. Send promotion package to those on mail list.	5 months
Receive local site brochures from convention bureau. Keep running list of mail-in registrants. Print rules; distribute to registration staff. Collate registration packets.	1 month
Have signage printed. Determine site equipment needs.	2 weeks
Arrange for refreshments/meals of staff. Close reservation list; type master list of attendees. Print name tags. Collect and deposit last of reservation fees.	1 week
Organize and pack needs.	1 day
Set up registration table and equipment. Begin registration. Keep event agenda accessible. Count money and bank. Extend hospitality to attendees.	Event day
Make notes on event evaluation and hold critique session. Execute final accounting.	Following event

Table 8 Convention Registration Needs

Convention Registration Equipment Needs

— Blank name tags
— Blank receipts
— Calculators
— Cash register/cash box
— Computers
— Copy machine
— Bulletin/marker boards
— Change (in proportion to
    event size and ticket price)
— Charge card machine and
    slips
— Change of address forms
— Erasers
— Fax machine
— First aid kit
— Glue
— Liability statements
— Lost and found box
— Markers
— Master registration list
— Message pads
— Name tags (alphabetical)

— Paper
— Pencil sharpener
— Pens and pencils
— Policy sheet
— Printers
— Programs
— Pushpins
— Registration packets
— Rubber bands
— Ruler
— Scissors
— Scratch pads
— Stapler
— Tape
— Telephones
— Tickets, hand stamps
— Typewriters
— Walkie-talkies

Financial Manager's Responsibilities

For conventions, trade shows and seminars, there are many important jobs for the person who is in charge of the finances. The list below spells out most of those jobs and responsibilities. Depending upon who the person is and how much direct responsibility he or she wants to have, the list could be a lot longer. This person is important, and the job requires a high degree of detail and responsibility. The financial manager must:

- Open official bank account
- Pay site deposit and other advance fees
- Figure preliminary budget with chairperson
- Determine fee schedule
- Mail invoices to exhibitors and attendees
- Pay bills, deposit fees
- Finalize budget
- Meet with committee
- Confirm all contracts
- Deposit last of advance registration fees
- Get final count of attendees
- Pick up small bills and change from bank
- Disperse money
- Collect and count money
- Deposit gate receipts
- Finish all budgetary paperwork
- Calculate profit and loss

Speaker Selection

Speakers can contribute greatly to the success of your convention, sales meeting or banquet. The following tips will help you achieve the maximum success from this investment of time and money:

— Determine your objectives and define the topics you want covered
— Speakers can be obtained from:
  • Special event management firms
  • Speakers bureaus
  • Universities
  • Professional peer recommendations
— To ensure your selection is right for your group:
  • Ask for a video or audio cassette
  • Ask for, and check, the most current references for similar occasions and audiences
  • Ask to attend their next presentation after confirming and signing a contract
— Send your selected speaker the following information in contract form:
  • Date, time and place of event
  • Fees agreed to, and what expenses will be paid
  • Topic and length of time agreed
  • Audience profile
  • Information on the group or company you are representing and the reason for the meeting
  • Theme of the event
  • Other speakers and their topics, if appropriate
  • Other details such as: room layout; dress for the occasion; meeting convention promotion pieces; request picture and biographical information; inform of airport pick-up; request list of special equipment, such as audio visual needs; request prepared introduction; send hotel and travel arrangements.

Innovative speakers generate motivation, boost morale and contribute practical, useful information. They can create the guests' desire to attend, and, depending on the individual's stature, can contribute to the overall event image.

Producing Printed Items

Once you have determined your theme for the event, you can begin the process of printing your collatoral materials.

A graphic artist is one of your first calls, so that an event logo can be designed. This graphic will be used on all of your printing to give continuity and professionalism to your project.

The following list will help develop an organized approach to this major task:

— **Establish a budget**
   Start with past budgets and compare current needs

— **Develop a list of printed items**
   Meeting announcements
   Booth sale promotions
   Preliminary programs
   Accommodation forms
   Attendee promotions
   Follow-up promotions
   Registration forms
   Name badges
   Tickets
   Note pads
   Napkins

— **Check the design of items to mail**
   Do they meet postal requirements?
   Do you have correct permits for return mail?
   Will stamps adhere to selected paper finishes?

— **Send bids to at least three printers**
   Be sure you are comparing apples to apples
   Get samples of their work
   Can you work with your assigned sales representatives?
   Do they have other services of benefit (i.e., handling)?
   Can they handle the size of your job comfortably?

Can artist and printer communicate well?
Get references and check thoroughly
What is their expected work load when your job will
   be in-house?
Get paper samples

When you begin production of your materials:

- Give the printer a list of needs and deadlines
- If using postal permits, be sure they are on the finished art
- Set dates for proofs and deadlines
- Be sure you or your artist is present for the printing of important pieces
- Always allow adequate production time
- Have your mail lists in order and labels ready
- Be extremely thorough in copy proofing

Table 10 Facility Research/Evaluation Form

Facility Research/Evaluation Form

Facility _____

Address_____

Accessibility _____

Contact _____ Telephone no. _____

Rent_____ Deposit _____When returned _____

Overtime fees _____

Reserve_____months in advance. Deposit due___months in advance.

Lighting_____Decor/colors _____

Union regulations_____

Kitchen location _____

Kitchen equipment _____

_____

Audio-Visual equipment _____

Easels_____Blackboard_____Screen_____

Electrical outlets _____

Tables_____Size_____Chairs_____Style_____

Podium _____Sound system _____

Banquet rooms _____

General meeting rooms _____

Other areas/description_____

Storage rooms _____

Restrooms _____

Alcohol restrictions _____

Security_____

Parking_____

Maximum fire capacity _____

Comments _____

_____

_____

Chapter
8

Trade Shows

CHAPTER 8

TRADE SHOWS
The Aisles of Success — Production or Participation

Participating in a Trade Show

For many manufacturers and service companies, the Trade Show is the best and most efficient means of reaching their customers. A trade show is simply a gathering of buyers and sellers under one roof — a modern equivalent of a "market day" or a town festival — to review, in one fell swoop, a whole industry's products, pricing and innovations for the year.

Trade shows are usually held in large exhibit halls, with the exhibitors divided into booths of controlled sizes. Exhibitors display their wares in their booth as they see promotionally beneficial. Sales people hosting the booth are advised of this marketing strategy. Buyers roam the exhibit hall, visiting booths, looking at products, gathering literature, and buying when the best opportunities present themselves.

There is more to successful booth planning than a simple presentation of products. As in all aspects of selling, pizzazz and creativity can make the difference.

A recent study by the Laboratory of Advertising Performance at McGraw-Hill Research estimated that every sales call costs approximately $230 and every qualified trade show follow-up lead costs approximately $106.89. The study concluded that a sale accomplished through a trade show is six times more cost-effective than a regular sale.

There is no trick to getting a good investment return on your trade show exhibit; a lot of hard work, but no tricks. Following are several things you need to accomplish to make your experience a profitable one.

Before you go into a trade show, make sure you know who is going to be there. Are you sure they are your targeted buyers?

Ask the show management for attendance breakdowns. And also talk to other exhibitors about the audience. Once you know the numbers of important people to expect, then you can set an objective.

An objective is determined by what you want to accomplish by the end of the trade show. How many people do you want to have talked to, how many people do you want to have sold to, and what kind of dollar volume do you want to realize at the end of the trade show?

How large a booth do you want to buy? One of the advantages of exhibiting in a trade show is that you can look as great as your competitor, even though you may be a much smaller organization. Through the use of props, space, giveaways and all of the elements of a trade show, you can compete on an equal level. It is up to you to make sure that you look more successful than your competitors. People like to associate with or buy from those who are successful.

Before the show opens, call your sales people together and have a discussion about your goals for the trade show. Be sure they know all of the prepared materials, and how to encourage people to come into the booth. Let them know the role they are expected to play. This is not unlike a coach pulling his team together before a big game.

Most trade show booths have a giveaway item to attract people into their booths. However, you need to be careful not to attract the wrong people with the giveaway. You are there to sell a professional item, skill or service. You need the opportunity to talk to the right people. If people are coming into your booth just to get a piece of candy, you won't have the time to devote to the serious shopper of your product.

Always consider the use of a hospitality room. This is an ante-room where you can entertain clients and potential clients, usually after trade show hours. It is there that you can go into greater depth about your product with your customer who is very serious and wants to know more.

The behavior of your people is extremely important. They should reach out to your customers and impart enthusiasm and sincerity. Friendly, enthusiastic hands held out to attendees going by communicate that this is the way we will treat you at our company.

It would be good to reward the people of your booth who are using this attitude, by rewarding or giving them special recognition at the end of each day. The days get very long, therefore something to motivate them to continue to be enthusiastic would be appropriate.

Try to get a list of the anticipated attendees to the show from the trade show management. Use this list to send out invitations for special presentations at the trade show, in your hospitality suite, or at your booth.

Always keep in mind that you are trying to attract the same audience that all the other booths in the show are after.

The appearance of the booth is another place to set yourself apart. The space should be attractive, neat, and feature your product.

It is very helpful to have a telephone in your booth, for business of course. It would be a hot line to your office to get answers for questions asked by people at the trade show, or to handle a customer's complaint immediately.

People love to see demonstrations at trade shows. This is an opportunity to prove the superiority of your product through an interesting visual example. But please, use the demonstration in a very professional manner; no girls in bikinis or gimmicks that are unrelated to your product. Always be professional.

Keep a constant eye on how your audience is responding to you, your booth and your people. Maybe you need to change something slightly to be more effective, push one product further forward on your demonstration table, change a sign or even change your theme every-day, which will make you look versatile. Use the product in a different way, or present it differently with color, costumes or music — do whatever it takes to make the audience look another time. Generally you have the same audience traveling a trade show for two or three days. If you can give them something new to look at, they will stop twice and talk twice as long. Be sure your booth personnel are both spirited and on top of everything. Also ask that they share their experiences with you at the end of the day, which could lead to a way of improving the booth operation for the next day.

After the show, sit down with your people to evaluate every-thing that happened. This is valuable because if you have a product that lends itself to being presented at the trade show, you want to do it with maximum efficiency and cost productivity. This can be done best by finding out where mistakes may have turned up.

The first impression, the initial 30 seconds, can make the difference in a sale, and the success of your booth. Your staff determines this to a large extent. Schedule your staff for no more than four hours of continuous booth duty each day. Longer periods can cause fatigue and poor performance. However, this doesn't apply to your demonstrations or other temporary show personnel that you have hired to assist your staff. They expect to work the entire day with reasonable breaks for lunch and so on.

Your staff should have proven people-to-people skills, plus good product and company knowledge. A clean and well dressed appearance is very important. As far as dress is concerned, a conservative policy is best.

Of course, in your exhibit booths there are some things that are not acceptable, such as cigarettes, gum, food and drink, or anything else that might divert the attention of your prospects. It is very distracting to see your booth nicely displayed, but then see a coffee cup with someone else's bright logo on it. Your eye goes right to those things. Sitting down on the job creates and transmits a lethargic attitude. Train your staff to move within the parameters of the exhibit whenever they are free, and to make eye contact with the people that are passing by. Help them feel comfortable about starting conversations with likely prospects, and encourage them to smile. Smiling makes all the difference in the world. And, of course, back to enthusiasm; enough cannot be said about the accomplishments of a sincerely enthusiastic individual.

Producing Trade Shows

Your company, association, or another type of group may be interested in *producing* a trade show. This is a time-consuming, detail-oriented endeavor, but one that can accomplish some very great things for the sponsoring organization.

As with any other event, there are many items to consider when organizing a trade show — the budget, promotion, theme, etc. However, as a trade show sponsor, it is necessary to recognize that there is one area which differs from other events: there are two audiences — exhibitors and the attendees. Both sectors must be addressed.

The financial structure of hosting a trade show is relatively simple. Revenue is created by selling exhibit space on a set fee basis, according to the amount of space reserved. Expenses begin with the pipe and drape, plus the table, chairs and a sign for the booths. The cost of the decorations will be established in advance and can be as simple or elaborate as desired. There will be two phases to the promotional material: the first objective is to attract potential booth exhibitors; the second is to attract attendees. Another cost is the labor that will be required to set up booths, do the electrical work and maintenance.

Choice of facility, naturally, is made according to how many people are expected to rent space and attend the event. Check on the availability of hotel/motel rooms and their prices, restaurants, parking, loading docks, and whether the facility is generally able to accommodate the extra burden on their staff. Check on whether the management of the facility will supply the tools and labor needed to set up the booths. If not, be sure to have someone available to handle these requirements.

When producing a trade show in combination with a convention, the facility will be a critical part of your determination of which hotel or convention area to utilize. If you are producing an independent trade show, you have the flexibility to research various hotels, convention sights or whatever other types of space might be available in your locality that would be large enough to accommodate your show.

Other items to take into consideration are the accessibility of the facility from the viewpoint of exhibitors/attendees; parking availability (free? paid?); loading docks for the convenience of the exhibitors and your decorator and a possible holding area for materials/ equipment which might have to arrive a few days prior to the show.

You will also want to give consideration to the floor plan of the exhibit area, and what kind of extra labor is available through the facility (electricians, etc.). Although your decorator will be on site prior to exhibitors arriving, you will still need the cooperation of the facility management to have personnel available to assist wherever needed.

When working with the facility to set dates for your trade show, you should also find out from them what will be coming out of the facility prior to your show going in, as well as what is coming in after you. If you are pinned to a tight schedule with the before and after exhibits, you will not have any maneuverable space to change any times for set-up or removal or allow for last-minute details. At this point you also need to find out any specific shipping or receiving requirements the facility may have.

You need to be sure (prior to signing any contracts) of all the fees charged by the facility. In some cases they charge a service fee per booth as well as the rental of the room. You don't want to find that out at the end of the trade show. All of your costs need to be taken into consideration when determining the fee to charge exhibitors. If you are charged a 15% fee on top of the room rental, you need to be aware of that prior to contacting potential exhibitors.

It is important to ask about the security arrangements by the facility from the time your exhibitors are going to be arriving until the time of the departure of the last one. You will need to find out about the insurance and liability agreements. You should inquire if there are any union contract requirements prior to your decorator or exhibitors arriving for set up.

When doing your site inspection, you need to note any kind of structures, columns, vents, ducts, and electrical outlets and amperage capabilities. All of these points will sooner or later surface as questions that you should have the answers to!

It is a good idea to get a schematic of the room you are utilizing so you can know the exact measurements of the area. This will be beneficial for both the decorator and the exhibit booth floor planning. If there is a unique angle or a specific area that needs special handling, you can find out ahead of time and work with it so it does not become a problem at the last minute.

When talking with the facility owner or manager, discuss his past experiences. This will help you to determine a "plan of action" to assist you, your decorator and exhibitors for a smooth and successful trade show.

A trade show is a major special event which requires a very good team of management and support people, as has been outlined in the earlier chapter on grand openings. You and your team will need to do a marketing analysis; you will have to consider the location of the facility; the promotion of the trade show; the selection of the trade show facility; the convention service company (the pipe and drape people); the attendance promotions; on-site operations; follow-up procedures; and, of course, the budget.

As with every event, you need to determine your goals, whether it is to promote an industry cause, to present an organization's product to the appropriate audience, or to enhance an image.

You will need to determine your market, who will profit from exhibiting at your trade show and the publicity reasons for attendance at your trade show.

Can you expect the trade show to be financially profitable? Yes (with my usual caveat), "If you do it right!"

Trade Show Budget

The financial structure of your trade show should be carefully and thoroughly developed. It is a simple budget to create because there are few elements of revenue and few areas of expense.

Your exhibit space will be a flat fee. Your cost per booth will vary with the displays and decor you choose to provide. The convention decorator will charge a flat fee per booth, and any other decorating elements they provide will be a known figure you can incorporate into expenses. Signage can also be provided by this vendor.

Registration costs include many forms and on-site equipment, such as word processors. Labor should be included as an expense. Basic printing expenses will be name tags and booklets or information packets that include a floor map of the booths, their numbers and names. You could also provide printed bags or promotional pieces, such as pencils, pads and buttons.

Attendance promotions are prizes for participating and winning special games intended to get people involved in each booth. These gifts can range from $5.00 to $5,000, depending on your audience and type of trade show.

If you are uncertain what to charge for your booths, look to the local convention bureau for help. They know booth space fees in various regions of the country. They can also give you information that relates to certain industries, as well as areas you can research to find more in-depth answers to your questions. The rule of thumb in developing any fee structure applies after all your investigations — find out all the definite facts, costs, competitive booth fees, etc., and then think about the next two factors: What do you need operationally, and what do you want in revenue, if any? The last big consideration is "What will the market bear?"

CASE STUDY VIII

A Chamber of Commerce sponsors a mini trade show monthly — 20 booths of businesses display their products or services in front of a highly "qualified-to-buy" audience.

The show's benefit to the Chamber is the demonstration of its service attitude toward the business community — which voluntarily chooses to support them or not!

Promotions from the Chamber to potential exhibitors originally required a traditional printed promotional piece stating the advantages and benefits of participation in the show. Due to the past success of these events, they no longer needed to promote their space. The show proved to be so productive for its exhibitors, the Chamber soon had a waiting list of three to four months. Similar organizations send out a sign-up sheet at the beginning of the year for their "table-top" exhibitors, and that response, plus on-going telephone sign-ups, fill the openings for their meetings. This is a good source of revenue for the organization.

The event coordinator for the Chamber arranged for the facility for the monthly meeting. It required enough space for the 20 booths and a stand-up reception for approximately 600 people. A good rule to follow is that the more unique the facility, the greater the attendance.

A new local hotel provided a good combination of space and curiosity to draw attendance. It was also a promotion for the hotel as well as the trade show.

The hotel's catering staff took care of the food. It was presented with style, which enabled the hotel to promote its ability to handle a function for any of the Chambers' guests.

The exhibitors were sent information on the date, place and time of set up after remitting the exhibit fee. Generally, such a fee is between $50 to $200, depending on the demand. The fee included tickets of admission which the exhibitors were able to use and give to clients. The ticket value, or cost of attendance, is approximately $5.

The convention decorators set up pipe, drape and skirted tables in each booth (all measured 10-foot x 10-foot). A sign with the company name was hung on the back drop of the booth.

Exhibitors came on-site to set up their displays two to three hours before opening. Any special needs were taken care of by the hotel staff during that time, such as electricity, water and equipment.

Drawings for prizes that were donated by the exhibitors were held periodically during the two hour show. This created excitment and a reason for the attendees to stay until the end, thus ensuring maximum exposure time for the vendors.

The guests networked with their business peers, and were able to ask questions about various products or services of interest to them. This was a good service in the eyes of those who do not like to take time from their busy day for vendor sales calls.

The trade show provided: exposure to Chamber members' businesses; the ability for attendees to network and see products and services they could use; revenue for the Chamber and good public relations benefits. The trade show was a "win-win-win" situation!

| CASE STUDY IX |

A medical convention included a vendor trade show as part of the conventioneers reason to attend the conference. The attendees perceive the new information they will receive to be very important to their business, as state-of-the-art knowledge always is.

This convention management saw the trade show exhibition as a means of revenue, a way to give financial substance to the three day event and as a service to its members.

The exhibitors recognized the value of the show because of the qualified group of buyers of their products. They could save thousands of dollars in sales calls by participating in this show. In addition, they had the opportunity of selling a large volume of goods or services.

The image enhancement of both the show sponsor and the vendor was very positive, and yet relative to their individual efforts and investments.

This was another "win-win-win" situation. The steps that our show management went through to develop, organize and execute the event were:

— Determination of goals
— Creation of theme
— Budget development
— Site selection and negotiation
— Promotion development, printing and mailing
— Research and hiring of necessary services
— Organization
— Show set-up and decorating
— Management of services
— Procurement of promotional items
— On-site execution
— Evaluation after event for improvement

The theme of this medical trade show was "A Golden Opportunity."

The "gold" created many verbal and visual options for us — the decorations, promotional graphics and copy, mixer games, and all the themed events.

An 8-foot tall pot of gold was created for the center of the exhibit hall. There were 16-foot gold glitter rods shooting up from the center, as well as ropes of golden lights. These lights were attached to the ceiling and rotated, creating a radiating effect from the pot to the ceiling. Gold rocks had been painted and glittered along with large bundles of paper "nuggets" for the top of the pot and around the base. In addition, gold glittered chicken wire flowed out and around the large pot. This large focal point was constructed on a stage covered with gold carpet. The company logo, painted gold, hung from ceiling to floor in the center of the radiating lights.

The opening of the trade show was done ceremoniously to develop an attitude of excitement and "specialness" about the show.

A 14-foot x 14-foot gold vault facade had been created for the entrance. Guests were led down a 20-foot gold carpet, containing gold glitter, to the vault doors, by the company president.

Live music was supplied creating further excitement, which also stepped up the pace of the group.

A large combination lock had been developed to use as part of the ceremony — with the "right combination" they could gain entrance to this vault — symbolic of riches to be found within . . . "a golden opportunity." As they passed through the doors, there were shelves on both sides of the vault, lined with "bags of gold" and "gold bars."

The house lights were down in the exhibit hall, and artifical smoke had been pumped into the room to surround the "pot-of-gold." The smoke allowed for greater reflection of the lights radiating from the golden pot.

Once the guests were inside the hall, the lights came up and they started down the rows of vendors to explore their "opportunities."

The exposure time to the booths had been carefully planned. Too much time can create an apathy about a show. Too little time frustrates exhibitors and attendees. This one hundred booth show had six hours total exposure over a two day period. Everyone found this time to be just right.

We had promised our vendors, in our promotion of the event, that part of their fee would be spent trying to maximize the attendees visits to their booths. "Games" for lack of a more professional word, were created for this goal. It takes a very creative team to sit down and develop such directed games. We used them on two occasions — the event reception held in the exhibition hall and with a brunch the next morning.

One game was the "planting" of a golden nugget in several booths — attendees were to hunt for this nugget and when found, its number on the bottom allowed the "finder" to come to the pot of gold for a prize. All the prizes were on display and had been purchased to match the demographics of the attendees. About $2,000 had been allowed in the budget for these gifts. Similar games can be developed according to your theme and guest profile.

On the first evening, a cocktail reception was planned right in the exhibit hall. People could casually walk around carrying food and drinks, talking to the vendors. The food tables and bars were strategically placed to promote movement about the hall.

The evening's theme was "A Treasure of Golden Rewards." The vault doors to the hall had been covered entirely by a huge pirate ship. There was a gang-plank to walk on-board the ship, surrounded by large ropes, barrels and other pirate paraphernalia.

A concertina player walked about the hall. A pirate with a pegged leg and a parrot on his shoulder hobbled about. The servers all wore pirate costumes and an emcee created further atmosphere with his high-seas pirate lingo and gold brocade costume. He kept the evening exciting by encouraging visitors to go from booth to booth to seek treasures.

The huge pot-of-gold was covered for this event by an even larger treasure chest. It was equally glittery and good looking. The decorator created it to fit onto and over the pot, so the radiating lights would appear to be coming from the treasure. It looked great!

Working with your decorator, using good communications, mutual respect and patience, produces a productive attitude. This is tremendously important. Without it you will not be able to implement your creative ideas, and you cannot do all of these things yourself!

These decorations, games and other elements may seem unnecessary, but if you are building an event that will enhance your company's image, bring people back next year, and create excitement and appreciation for the show — it is important! It requires creativity, time and money, but it is a good investment. If all these things are working for you, you will be able to raise your booth fees, which increases your revenue.

At the morning session of the trade show you assume the attendees have seen all the booths from four hours the day before. This means being creative again, developing reasons for moving from booth to booth. Note here that the show manager is responsible for getting the buyers to the vendors — the vendors have to do their creative things to get them to stop and hear a sales pitch. You should make them aware of this responsibility and need. We offered a best booth award in several categories, to increase the vendors' desire to look good. This prize was a discount on next year's booth fees, to encourage their return.

Breakfast/brunch was served in the exposition hall. It was delicious and well presented, giving a further message of quality to the event. The tables were again distributed well so the vendors could share the attention of the group — people tend to hover around food and drink areas.

Our emcee was back to brighten the morning and encouraged the audience to go to all the booths. He explained and verbally handled the motivational games. Our staff checked winners and handed out prizes.

The promotion of such a trade show needs to be carefully, creatively and thoroughly executed. Your goal is to motivate participation, establish the high standard of the trade show and be regarded above the competition. Always be aware of the competition for trade show dollars. Organizations are beginning to recognize its huge revenue potential.

Your graphic type, color and selection are so important — get the best artist you can afford. It is an important investment into your trade show image. Printed pieces establish the first impression of your event. If it looks like you scrimped and cut corners, the reader will feel that is what he will get at the show. If, in contrast to your competition, you promote your event using quality paper with gold embossing, as we did with "The Golden Opportunity," yet charging about the same fees to the same audience, then it's no contest — you win! People will always go with the obvious "winners!"

Copy writers are great, but they must understand your goals, message and audience. We have copy writers on staff to ensure this understanding, thus creating greater success.

You must include so many details beyond date, time and place, such as speakers you may be bringing in, special events surrounding exhibit hours, other exhibitors, fees and space definition, to name a few.

Your exhibition decorator will help you with the registration form. It contains the proper legal terminology and all the rules, regulations, responsibilities and requests for additional equipment. This needs to be carefully considered from the viewpoint of all parties, and then reviewed by your attorney, as liabilities are defined in this document.

Negotiations with your facility must also be well documented and clearly understood — you do not want surprises, you do want profits, or at least to stay within your planned budget.

The fee you charge for each exhibit booth is yours to determine. Look at industry standards, value received, and what the market will bear. Remember, the more you give (value), the more you will receive!

Your exhibition decorator will handle the drayage (the exhibit booth facades, props and set-ups) for your vendors. Depending on when it is sent, if more than a week before set-up date, it can be directed to their warehouse for shipping on the proper day. If materials arrive right before the exhibit, the facility will receive and store them for your people.

Set-up day will be primarily handled by your exhibition decorators. They put up a booth for themselves from which they operate, in view of all the vendors, so vendors will know where to go for equipment or services.

They put up all the pipe and drapery needed, creating the 10-foot x 10-foot booths, as an example, in the places you represented them to be. They can also make signs, in advance of the show, and put them on the back of the booth to identify the exhibitor.

This is true of teardown also. The convention decorator — who in my opinion wears a shiny halo (we need these guys, and our selected company is great) — are there to assist with this process, including the drayage, shipping, handling and storage if necessary. They charge for all of these services, of course.

We have covered the goal determination, theme creation, site

selection, negotiations, decor, motivational attendance games, the set-up and removal and more. After the execution of all your efforts, the event is over, and it is time for critique and evaluation.

Your vendors and attendees have already participated in this process, hopefully through printed

Information exchange plus business development and enhancement can be accomplished at conventions, motivational meetings, seminars and trade shows.

forms and your request for opinions. Using these as guidelines, your staff needs to discuss openly the pros and cons of how the various elements worked and went together. The purpose of this exercise is obviously to see if you want to do it again — when and how? What changes will need to be made to make it better? Are fees in order? Do you need to change your budget in various areas?

Trade shows can be very rewarding. They are often the reason to get and retain interest and membership in your organization. Attendance at meetings or conventions is enhanced with the anticipation of a showing of new products or special offerings from exhibitors. Trade shows require tremendous work, money and labor to be done well — and they *must* be done well, with careful planning, execution, creativity and professionalism. If you are inexperienced, you will add five years to your life if you pass the job to a consultant or professional manager!

Chapter
9

Sales Meetings

CHAPTER 9

SALES MEETINGS
The Means to Motivational Methods

There are various types of sales meetings, but the two that will be discussed here are: sales meetings held by large corporations, and conventions. The goals are essentially the same for both — to get and hold the attention of the participants and accomplish some important sales tasks in a very short period of time.

Because sales meetings are an essential part of a company, they are special events in themselves, and they are treated by management as *investments*. They must be educational and productive, but they also must be creative with one objective being to produce enthusiasm. The potential of sales meetings is great, in that they can influence the direction of your organization for the future.

Sometimes sales meetings are also for relaxation and recreation, but that part of the agenda occurs only after the work is done or the purpose of the meeting is accomplished. The desired results on the part of the meeting planners is to create a positive attitude that will motivate people "to keep up the good work."

The most effective method of getting results is by creating a theme that ultimately maintains enthusiasm and good company feelings over the year.

The value of meetings is in the opportunity they provide for communication, one of the main roads to success. The following are suggestions on how to begin planning a sales meeting:

— Set the goals of the meeting
— Develop a direction/concept
— Develop a theme
— Know your audience
— Define the message

When planning the meeting, the first thing to do is preset the attitude of your attendees. You can do this in the promotional material that is sent out prior to the meeting: a teaser before the participants leave home to build anticipation, project a hearty welcome and create an enthusiastic beginning to your meeting even before it begins. In addition, the printed material will give the time, place, dates and other pertinent information.

Management will develop an agenda which will include who will be speaking, when they will speak, the sequence of input, time allotment, and the subject matter on which they will speak. Speakers need to be a part of the early stage of planning so that their needs and fees can be taken into account in the overall budget.

Speaker selection should be done by communication ability and content first, and fee second. A friend of mine, Joe Bonura, an excellent professional speaker, reminds me of his answer when asked about his fee: "You should want to spend at least as much money feeding their minds as you do per person on their food — you've brought them together to teach them."

It is important that the lay-speaker spends an appropriate amount of time in developing an interesting presentation. This may mean that the use of audio visuals or technical equipment may be needed, if the budget allows. When professional speakers are hired they will give you all their requirements, such as monitors, projectors, etc.

The site selection of your meeting is based on what you want to accomplish and the size of your audience. Because your aim is to motivate and inspire confidence that your organization is strong, the site must be the best that your budget allows. This is an investment in your image.

A conference room can be adequate for your needs, if it is comfortable and well equipped. Today, conference rooms are very well designed for all the psychological needs of meeting participants. These rooms and facilities cost a little more, but if they can make your total presentation more effective, they are worth the extra investment.

Check your potential facility to make sure there will be no ringing telephones, music systems, or outside noises that could interfere with the meeting. Two real "bugaboos" of mine are noisy chairs and squeeky doors. These detract from the presentor and presentation.

If the audience is larger than 100 people and they may be asking questions, provide floor microphones for the question-and-answer period.

There are understandably some meetings that must stick to business only — to make a point, or get the work done. However, for building acceptance and anticipation for meeting attendance, the recreational capabilities of your selected site can be promoted. In that case, time should be allotted within your agenda for your participants to take advantage of the facilities. Free time is usually allowed in the late afternoon.

Meals are an important part of a successful meeting. The facility selected should be capable of producing fine food, as usually there is nothing else available other than what is prepared at the convention site. It is interesting to note how often an entire meeting or convention is judged by the food that is presented, so consider spending a good portion of the budget on good meals. Any food that is not included in the registration fee should be affordable. Often hotels or resorts will have at least two types of dining facilities: a formal dining room and the less expensive, informal coffee shop.

Start each day with enthusiasm. The powerful "Good Morning" by your first speaker or management representative might sound trite, but a weak approach will give your meeting a weak start. Tell the participants that this is going to be a *great* meeting; tell them enthusiastically and on an on-going basis. It works!

The importance of good speakers has already been discussed, but remember, whether they are management or professionals, the content of their speeches must be excellent. This is your motivational opportunity — the *package* you are presenting has to be exceptional.

Have exciting breaks that refresh people both physically and mentally. Most people look forward to a cup of coffee, soft drinks, or juice at a break. It is fine to provide them with that sort of refreshment, but what about a surprise? One favorite of ours is a soda fountain with an attendant who prepares milk shakes to order with quality products, including fresh bananas, strawberries, and blueberries.

Depending on your theme, this might be a good opportunity for a little recreation time. For instance, if your emphasis is on sports, a basketball tournament using miniature equipment might be appropriate. Some participants could play, some could be cheerleaders, some scorekeepers, and so on. This kind of play tends to divert the mind completely from the material presented, creating a more relaxed atmosphere. It also contributes to the total attitude and teamwork of the meeting, which is the ultimate goal. Once the participants are back in their seats, refreshed and full of energy, they are ready to be presented with more material.

A relaxed lunch is another opportunity to develop the purpose of the meeting and to re-present the participants with the idea that the special efforts that went into the meeting were made for them because they are special and valuable. Lunchtime should also include some free time. Sales people need to have the use of the telephone in order to check in with their clients.

The middle of the afternoon session is an appropriate time to have another exciting break. Because of the morning break and lunch, the participants will expect something great, so pull out all the stops and do something special for them. Incorporate the unusual, such as fun activities that would include animals, props and music. After the break, it's back to the meeting room for the final gathering of the day. Usually the afternoon meetings are dismissed between 4:00 and 5:00 so the participants have time to relax, either in their rooms or by participating in the recreational facilities available.

During the day, or at the evening banquet, create an opportunity for some form of awards presentation. Entertainment can be included, perhaps with a skit involving the meeting participants. It will take a little extra time to plan this type of program with actors or association members, but it is well worth the effort. It will create memories and topics of conversation for years to come. Or you might consider a more elaborate gala with well-known talent or a dinner dance. Even though the participants may pay for this event, it is still a memorable occasion.

The length of the meeting depends on the total meeting agenda and the ability of the participant to be away from their business or homes. Generally, a sales meeting lasts one or two days, and a convention lasts from two to four days. No matter how long the meeting, the wrap-up should be dynamic. You may not see these people again for another year, so your message must be filled with memorable information that will be important to them in their work or enable them to recapture a good impression about the company . To present a positive, lasting impression, you will want to end on an enthusiastic note. If the participants feel good about the time they have invested in coming to the meeting, it will have been successful.

CASE STUDY X

The goal of the client for its annual sales meeting was to recognize the efforts of the sales staff and to motivate them to continue doing their best work, or to be "Super Heros."

We used a theme which was an ingredient of the Japanese work culture and a positive nostalgic part of our childhoods — the popular super hero of the comic book. The company's name was used in the theme title, "Rosco to the Rescue." It underscored the company's commitment to quality service. It also highlighted the important role the sales staff played in keeping their customers satisfied.

The message the employees were to take away with them was the company's appreciation for the superior service they had given their customers all year. Because of the excellent job they had done, Rosco Tents had grown more and been more profitable than ever before; and, through teamwork, determination, and continued good customer relations, Rosco Tents would undoubtedly surge ahead in the coming year.

Meeting topics were suggested, based on the Rosco mission statement and other company background information.

We looked for unusual awards that would back up our "Super Hero" theme. These awards were to be distributed throughout the year, a technique that continually supports the original statement.

The meeting was held at a local hotel. Beginning on a Friday evening in a casual atmosphere, the participants talked to one another about their experiences over the past year.

On Saturday morning they gathered for an early breakfast. Thematic comic books were on the table with an enclosed agenda for the day. "Super Hero" buttons doubled as name badges.

Business meeting topics were based on the theme, "Teamwork." A logo of a Super Hero flying through the air was developed for the event, with the "Rosco to the Rescue" title included in the logo. Brightly colored pads and a pencil printed with the event logo were at each person's place.

During the first break, high energy granola bars were served, as well as "Super Hero" bubble gum and other snacks. "Super Hero" masks were handed out for fun. The props around the room, an eight foot inflated Superman with the company logo on his chest and a gigantic poster, also reinforced the theme.

Back in the meeting room, the discussions were about "Beating the Villain" at his own game and "How to Triumph Over the Competition," all in keeping with the theme.

At lunch there was "Kryptonite" on the tables as well as miniature Super Heros for centerpieces. Lunch consisted of *hero* sandwiches. There was a motivational speaker following lunch whose topic was "Being Forthright and Strong" in one's daily efforts.

The afternoon meeting topics were, "Is it a bird? Is it a plane? No, it's a customer," "How to Woo Potential Customers," and "How to Keep Current Customers Satisfied."

The next break was a "Power Break," with sundaes from a sundae bar, and hero tee-shirts were distributed to the attendees.

The final meeting topic was "Shazam!" or "The Future Belongs to Rosco Tents," "What Lies Ahead," and "How Can We Capitalize on Our Opportunities?"

Guests at the cocktail hour that followed were greeted by pulsating lights that created a dramatic effect. The room was decorated with colorful balloons and "Super Hero" memorabilia. Taped music of "Super Hero" theme songs played while old "Super Hero" movies were shown on a large screen television. Exciting table centerpieces incorporated sculptures of "Super Heros" and neon lights.

In the dining area there was a telephone booth near the stage, which was draped in multicolored curtains. After dinner, the guest speaker, a villainous, sinister looking character began his remarks. As the participants listened, they began to realize that his advice was contrary to the training that the Rosco salespeople had received. The ominous mood was accentuated by lights dimming and the rising tone of the speaker's voice. Suddenly, another character who had been seated in the audience and dressed as a mild-mannered, anonymous salesperson challenged the speaker. (The challenger had been seen occasionally throughout the day at meetings and breaks). The salesman leaped from the crowd and disappeared into the telephone booth. With flashing lights, smoke, and music, "Captain Rosco" emerged

Themes can be originated from popular trends in advertising or television. The "Back to Basics" concept, modeled after the Bartles & Jaymes commercials, produced the theme for this annual sales meeting.

from the booth dressed as a "Super Hero." The villain made a quick exit and "Captain Rosco" made brief motivational remarks. Finally, the super hero and his pals sang a song with lyrics about the Rosco Tents' sales staff. "Captain Rosco" later returned to help with the awards: large Kryptonite sculptures with commemorative brass plaques, noting the recipient's achievements.

The meeting surpassed our goals! It ran smoothly, on time and the facility was perfect. The meals were very good and the attendance was excellent. Information developed and presented by management was obviously well received and absorbed. The elements of fun and decor added the enthusiasm, motivation and overall image building we were trying to accomplish. The sales staff returned to their territories feeling like "Super Heros" who could sell anything to anyone and that service was their middle name!

Chapter
10

Awards Banquets

CHAPTER 10

AWARDS BANQUETS
Professional Procedures to Acknowledge Performance

People in all walks of life enjoy and need appreciation for their efforts. A formal celebration for workplace or professional accomplishments can take the form of an annual Awards Banquet. Those who have worked hard anticipate with pleasure the recognition for their job well done. Because there is so much pride and happiness at stake, an awards banquet should be grand — as grand as your budget will allow.

If the awards banquet is held concurrently with the annual sales meeting or convention, it is best if the banquet follows the overall theme of that meeting. Create a celebratory ambiance for the event, with fine food, decor and entertainment. Make it look as though you have gone to great expense and trouble to make this a *special event*. When it is time for the actual awards presentation, do so with ceremony. Music with a fanfare or a jubilant march will create the right atmosphere.

An unusual trophy for the honored recipients will let these winners know that you wanted to make an extra effort to recognize their accomplishments. A symbol could be made, such as a sculpture depicting a figure that is pertinent to either the company's product or name, or reflective of the association. Perhaps a trophy could be designed and given year after year, something that would be identifiable in the industry when displayed by the recipients.

The awards presentation, perhaps with a champagne celebration, can be rewarding itself! This can be a time for peers to congratulate each other. Have a photographer on hand to take pictures, then use the photographs in a follow-up press release to local media, or for your company newsletter.

The awards banquet is created following the same elements listed in Chapter 3 for designing the grand opening celebration:

— Creative sessions for the concept and theme
— Budget development
— Research of necessary services
— Site determination
— Implementation of event
— Bookkeeping
— Critique

Obviously, the awards banquet will have its own set of considerations to be planned, such as:

— Identifying potential recipients
— Judging to determine the winners
— Scripting the ceremony
— Designing the type of award to present
— Using visual effects — slides or video
— Rehearsing — a must!

If the awards banquet is a fundraiser, (and they certainly can be profitable), then you will be developing a mini business plan:

— Goals
— Projected expenses
— Projected revenues
— Projected profits

Within a fundraiser is the issue of promotion expense and ticket sales. Be realistic here, or you could end up in a negative revenue situation that is unpleasant to all involved.

Awards banquets can be excellent public relations tools. By writing and sending a press release with a good "hook" to the local media and professional publications, press coverage can provide excellent publicity for the company.

The in-house benefits of such an event are long and far-reaching. Motivation to strive for excellence is an important result of the awards banquet for both associations and corporations of all sizes.

CASE STUDY XI

The Entrepreneur Society uses the awarding of trophies to deserving companies for two purposes: first and foremost, to embellish the Society's positive image and credibility, and second, to motivate the business community to achieve excellence.

The first stage of the event involved pulling the Society's committee together, determining their talents and, finally, hiring an events management firm to pull every element together and project a professional image, which was part of their goal.

Committees established included:

— Finance/Budget
— Publicity
— Facility
— Printing
— Decorations
— Entertainment
— Judges and Trophies
— Sponsorships

A creative session determined the concept, which was "Heralding the Exceptional Entrepreneur." Three long trumpets were used in the logo graphic with the theme copy beautifully scribed and included to enhance the total image.

This design was used on the invitations, printed napkins, banners, signage, the tropies and all promotional materials, including billboards.

The selected hotel ballroom was quite large, but going into the event, we didn't know how many people to expect, and we wanted the expansion capability. If we had stated on our promotions a location with a small ballroom, we would have had to limit our audience. To compensate for the large room, we decided to divide it into three sections with white and gold drapery, which added to the elegance of the evening.

The guests arrived in the lobby where they picked up their name badges and paid their ticket fees. There were signs giving credit to the sponsors, naming the nominees and welcoming all.

At the designated time, three formally-costumed trumpeters stood at the entrance to the ballroom and, with pomp and circumstance, sounded their trumpets inviting everyone to enter the first area, where the cocktails and hors d'oeuvres were being served.

Food stations were placed about the room with a variety of fine foods. This approach allowed a great networking of the attendees, and the crowd really enjoyed its uniqueness. The traditional sit-down dinner banquet can be overdone when some professionals have to attend several a week.

At the next designated time, the trumpeters appeared again, sounding the elongated gold instruments, which called the group to the second area. This was a formal auditorium with staging, podium, lighting and rows of seating for all.

In this atmosphere, dignitaries, Society members and guests paid tribute to the winning "entrepreneurs of the year."

A guest speaker, the Editor-in-Chief of *Inc.* magazine, George Gendron, discussed entrepreneurism. To close this portion of the program, the trumpets sounded for the finale, calling the guests to the third area. They walked through an 8-foot x 8-foot tunnel of gold, silver and white balloons with mylar streamers which touched their heads as they proceeded, creating interactive involvement.

The champagne celebration included elaborate desserts and coffees elegantly displayed. A brass ensemble created a further festive and jubilant atmosphere, where all the winners were congratulated and the press could film and interview.

The public relations, advertising and general publicity of the event was one of the largest expenses. There is no set percentage of cost to predictable revenue, because each event is different. The goals will determine the amount that will return what is necessary.

The decorations usually are florals at the head table where the dignitaries will be sitting and something simple on each dining table. Note the word "usually." In planning, try to reach out and attempt something really unique. If the banquet is remembered and talked about in another group of people at another time, you are getting a greater return on your investment. For example, the white and gold drapery dividing the rooms was non-traditional and effectively exciting. The trumpets, in keeping with the theme, were incorporated into the food stations along with flowers, greenery and ribbon.

Greenery set off the staging in the auditorium, along with a very large cutout of the Society logo behind and above the podium.

In addition to the balloon tunnel, there were gold, white and clear balloons covering the floor in the celebration room. An 8-foot x 8-foot glitter cut-out of the event logo was hung on the back wall and surrounded by gold drapery. This area was perfect for photos.

The decorations were very unusual for such an event, but the event was also unusual. It was judged to be very successful and the "best awards banquet ever" by many on the banquet circuit. They appreciated the fresh approach.

Chapter 11

Sales Promotions

CHAPTER 11

SALES PROMOTIONS
Producing Effective and Creative Campaigns

Sales promotions command attention when presented through powerfully produced special events, thus creating exceptional return on a company's marketing investment.

Competition today demands that everyone, from the manufacturer to the sales clerk, do all they can do to get a customer's positive response. This requires energy and creativity mixed with sophisticated research, marketing and promotions.

The initial research involves a few questions:

— What are the demographics of the target audience?
— What will appeal to this group?
— What are your needs and goals?
— Do you want the results to be fast-acting or long-lasting, bringing customers in gradually?
— Is it best held in or on the grounds of your facility; or would it seem more credible elsewhere?
— What is the budget, and what is the required return on this investment?

The answers to the above questions will be helpful in your creative session, which is next. The concept or type of event can be developed by evaluating your past experiences, your market, and often your competition's approach to sales.

Automobile dealers, recreational equipment dealers and furniture stores very often have outside tent or warehouse sales. Their colorful tents draw attention and people to their facility, the underlying promise being "Come here for a bargain."

Putting some pizzazz into those promotions would undoubtedly produce far more excitement, people, and sales. There is also the added possibility of publicity through media coverage of the "curiosity" you are staging.

So, pull your creative team together and let ideas flow. Remember, nothing negative, respect all ideas in the beginning, and weed out the ones that won't work later. Look for that special hook to help build your success. Then capsulize the promise of "what's in it for the customer or attendee" in an exciting and descriptive theme.

Research the costs of your selected promotion. Be sure to include printed support materials, and probably some advertising, to create awareness for your event. Lastly, promotional items, giveaways or prizes, special entertainment groups, and possibly food, are all budgetary considerations and event enhancements.

Today's consumers are continually bombarded with commercial pleas in so many forms. I am convinced the *special sales promotional event* is the most effective sales tool of all. Remember:

— Define your goals and customers
— Get customers' attention in a promotional invitation/announcement
— Recognize that the attendees are there because they are interested in what you are selling; prepare your approach accordingly
— If they do not buy this time, you know you have impressed them with positive information and a service attitude for their purchases at another time
— You also have had the opportunity to dispell misconceptions about your product/service, through this one-on-one communication

CASE STUDY XII

A large equipment retailer wanted to promote a new line of backhoes and trailers, as well as bring attention to its regular equipment inventory. Our creative concept answered their need, and it ultimately proved to be an effective sales event.

The theme of the sales promotion was "Colonial's Presidential Parade of Quality Equipment." This was held over a national holiday, using a red, white and blue patriotic approach.

Promotional flyers in the form of presidential proclamations were sent to their customer list of 3,000 names. A large ad was purchased for the newspaper, as well as some radio announcements to encourage the attendance of the general public.

Our client's facility was gigantic, allowing us the space to stage an indoor parade! We had stilt-walkers, bands, clowns, lots of balloons, and a review of Colonial's fine equipment. The features were highlighted enthusiastically at the microphone by the Sales Manager, assisted by "Uncle Sam," as each piece drove by the crowd.

The large warehouse was decorated much like Disney's "Main Street, USA," to emit an attitude of fun and welcome to the very large crowd. There were facades of store fronts, sidewalks and lamp posts. Costumed people stood about as live props, adding color and fun.

We served the all-American hot dogs and soft drinks and the guests took home small American flags. In addition, four lucky couples won trips to Washington, D.C., to see the presidential inauguration. Everyone left with a positive memory about Colonial Equipment Company.

Our client shared his success story with us later in the year. Company sales had doubled monthly for five straight months after this promotional sales event. This is only one of many events that have recorded such effectiveness.

Chapter
12

Fundraisers

CHAPTER 12

FUNDRAISERS
How to Maximize Effort While Minimizing Expenses

Fundraisers are generally held by non-profit organizations as a means of revenue. Corporations might also put forward a fundraising effort on behalf of a non-profit organization or an individual.

The first step in fundraising is to isolate the purpose. Perhaps there is an expensive piece of equipment that needs to be purchased for a special need. That amount might represent the goal of the event. With that in mind, the next thing to do is to look at the management structure available, and from there determine the number of volunteers needed to reach the goal. Whether for a non-profit organization or for a corporation, the volunteers are the means by which the major tasks are accomplished. The project must be very exciting in order to attract good volunteers. Management must also be committed, as occasionally a volunteer must drop out and someone in management has to take on the volunteer's responsibility.

The date and time are determined next. Your selected date and time will need to be checked to be certain that no other events will coincide with the fundraiser. Time conflicts with other events in the community will surely dilute the attendance and, therefore, the revenue.

After need, management structure, date, and time have been established, the next decision is to select the appropriate kind of event. Types of fundraisers include auctions, luncheons, bazaars, exhibits, concerts, balls, lawn parties, theatre benefits, fashion shows, testimonial banquets, and sporting events. All of these give patrons the opportunity to have a good time and, in most cases, make a tax-deductible contribution to a favorite cause. It is helpful to know some general information on each kind of fundraiser: Why does it succeed or fail? What does your community respond to best? What segment of the community supports the kind of event planned and the sponsoring organization? What size event is the staff capable of handling? How many volunteers can be recruited? Would a celebrity draw a larger audience and greater ticket price, and if so, who?

Let's go back to the tax deductible issue for quick clarification — not that the rules will not change, but some simple guidelines are offered by the Council of Better Business Bureau: "The purchase price of tickets to a fundraising dinner, circus or other meal or entertainment event is not fully deductible. Only the portion of the ticket price above the value of the meal or entertainment can be deducted for income tax purposes."

Three kinds of fundraisers which require an enormous amount of planning are telethons, marathons, and contests. They tend to raise large amounts of money and are more often covered by the media, but they need large groups of volunteers and, in some cases, must rely on people with specialized technical knowledge.

A good example of a fundraiser that traditionally is popular, will attract volunteers, and will have a reasonable profit margin is a charity ball. The planning begins just as it does with other special events — with a committee of creative people who will come up with a concept for a fun and successful evening. As always, an exciting theme is the first step. Next, it is important to choose the facility and the activities.

A budget needs to be set and ticket price determined. In general the expenses include: the facility, promotion of the project, printing the tickets and programs, decorations, musical entertainment, refreshments, souvenirs, labor, and miscellaneous expenses. For the sake of discussion, let's say a reasonable estimate would be between fifteen and twenty thousand dollars in cost. Added to that amount is the total money needed for the charity. If, for instance the two add up to seventy-five thousand dollars, the ticket price can be set by dividing that amount by the total number of people expected to attend. Another methodology of determing the projected gross revenue is multiplying the proposed expenses by four. (This is not scientific — only a rule of thumb!) The price per ticket also determines how grand the event must be in order to meet the expectations of the ticket holders.

Invitations, as the initial promotional piece, should be carefully designed because they preview what the recipient can expect at the event. The printer can be very helpful both in selection and cost (they will often donate all or part of the cost in exchange for having the company name somewhere on the invitation). It is preferable to hand-address the invitations, especially for a formal event. Naturally, the more creative and attractive the invitation, the more successful the response.

The mailing list might be generated from the organization's established supporters. If a special event management firm is being used, they may have names of philanthropic support groups.

A word of caution: too many fundraisers can be time-consuming and expensive, in addition to being poorly attended. However, once an event has been successfully established, it can be repeated on a yearly basis, and have a dependable audience and revenue.

A short review of the elements to consider for a successful chairty ball fundraiser are as follows:

— Determine financial goals
— Form management and volunteer committees
— Create a concept that allows opportunities to promote enthusiasm among the workers and guests
— Determine the time and place of the fundraiser, avoiding the holidays and considering other fundraisers that could compete with the chosen date and time
— Plan thoroughly and assign jobs
— Determine and evaluate the budget
— Establish a convenient time for all of the committee meetings
— Send a list of requirements to all vendors — keep a copy to refer to later
— Continually motivate the volunteer staff
— Approximately ten days before the event make a thorough checklist of all the vendors and make sure they are all ready
— Evaluate any potential problems
— Two days before the event run through the checklist again
— When the day arrives, motivate the staff and stay calm
— Check off vendors as they arrive
— Allow time for rest before the event begins

— Manage the sequence of planned elements with calm objectivity

Relax and enjoy your successful event!
Now on to a fun case study of a charity ball!

CASE STUDY XIII

I am going to describe a charity ball that I did for an organization *before* I became a professional event manager. The number of hours I put into this project went far beyond what a corporation or an organization would be able to pay for a management firm!

The name of the charity ball was "TARA," referring to the Southern plantation of Scarlet and Rhett. We created 18-foot tree trunks in my basement out of papier maché. The two tree trunks were taken to the hotel ballroom. Real branches with leaves were attached to the trunks and to the ceiling, creating huge trees in the ballroom — the effect was absolutely magnificent. The committee volunteers had been collecting Spanish moss for the trees six months prior to the charity ball.

A funny note on those 18-foot trees — and my lack of experience. First of all, my husband told me the project could not be done. That was my source of determination/motivation throughout the six months it took to build the four tree halves. (Yes, in order to get them out the basement doors, we planned ahead — thanks again to my husband, who cut the 6-foot round metal frames in half.) The trees were made of graduated sizes of metal frames, nailed to 18-foot 2 x 4s, then covered with chicken wire.

I then set out to make the papier-maché paste, buying a five pound bag of flour. By the time I finished, I had worn a path to the grocery store. It took seventy-five pounds of flour and months of newspapers and a vat to mix the paste properly! I loved doing it, though. Anyone interested in such an endeavor should know that the Sunday magazine is excellent for the exterior bark of trees!

This is an example of what can be done on a shoe-string budget. Today, if an adequate budget were available, we would use a "prop" tree from any number of decorators or theatrical prop houses.

Large iron gates from an antique salvage company and numerous plants from a local nursery were combined with hundreds of dogwood trees we had made from tree branches. Painted forty foot scenes of the Southern countryside, with hills, large trees, a gazebo and such were placed on each side of the entrance to the ballroom. They were skirted by the donated plants, helping to create a more dimensional look. A mansion backdrop was painted to hang behind the band.

Thematic centerpieces were advantageous for people to see and feel something tangible of the event as they were sitting at their table.

An area was set aside to allow for memorable photographs to be taken. (If negotiated properly with a professional photographer, pictures can be a revenue producer for an organization.)

The orchestra was one of the reasons people attended this event. There was entertainment along with music, giving the event an additional selling point and the ability to increase the ticket price.

Anything can be accomplished if you put your mind to it! Two artificial 18-foot trees like this one were made by hand.

Chapter
13

Holiday Events

CHAPTER 13

HOLIDAY EVENTS
Creating Outrageously Celebratious Happenings

Holiday events of any season or reason should be festive but professional for either businesses or professional organizations. They are usually produced for public relations purposes, so we're talking about preserving or enhancing a positive image. Therefore, the whole staff must realize the organization's objectives and that they are to use their best professional manners. The clearest way to remember the goal is to refer to the gathering as an *event* rather than a party.

Local festivals, as well as holidays, create reasons to plan an event. These occasions are so large and exciting, people naturally want to attend the activities. Such times are of particular benefit to organizations, because people are already in a festive mood. Corporations can use this time to bring clients in from other parts of the country. The prestige of some events contributes to the positive image of the host.

The reasons for holiday or festival functions are as varied as types of businesses and associates, but basically the purpose is the same: to get more business; to project an image which will help in retaining old clients and attracting new ones; to raise money by having a fundraiser at a time when people are already in a relaxed, receptive mood; to entertain participants in a sales meeting . . . and more.

In planning, the initial steps apply as with most special events: goals are determined; the participants are established; the message is outlined; and a theme is developed. Previously mentioned methods of organizing and implementing should be followed (see Chapter 3), including the development of a theme, budget, research, hiring services, implementation and critique.

Hints for Holiday Events

Take advantage of the opportunity to have a corporate or organizational event that coincides with a national holiday or a local festival. For instance, during the festivities leading up to the Indy 500, Kentucky Derby or Mardi Gras there are usually celebrities attending some or all of the events. They might be included in invitations to events, such as a grand opening, to see the new facility. Their presence will attract more media coverage which could even be picked up by a national wire service.

Make your event "top notch." Establish a theme that coincides with the expectations of the guests. The food and decorations should reflect the theme and the holiday that the event is celebrating. Checkered flags, for example, could be used for an Indy 500 party, along with spring flowers. Traditional Kentucky food and mint juleps, in abundance would be on the menu for a Derby party.

When entertaining people from different parts of the country and celebrities, try to arrange the food, drinks and entertainment so that everyone mingles. The more people come in contact with each other, especially when they are from different cities and backgrounds, the more successful the event will be. Word will spread far and wide about an elegant and fun event.

If the festivities are to be held over a period of a few days, the guests should be entertained from the time they arrive until they depart. Limousines are often hired to transport people from place to place. They should be stocked with food, beverages and flowers when possible. Hotel accomodations are expensive, limited, and usually must be made well in advance (in Louisville at Derbytime a year is not too soon). Gifts, such as flowers, fruit, candy, and baskets of goodies are traditionally placed in the guest's room. When available, the gift should reflect the holiday or the theme of the event.

Restaurants are generally crowded during these times, so reservations are a must. Take into consideration the guests' tastes, and let the restaurant know in advance if special needs must be accommodated. Order flowers or a centerpiece for the table. Special rooms can be arranged for privacy or when special entertainment is planned.

There are many fun-filled events going on during fesitval

periods in which guests like to participate. Each of the events show the flavor and attitude of the community, which tends to enhance the overall image of the event, and the ability for everyone to be caught up in the excitement.

Guests often know something about the city they are visiting, and they may want to "see the sights." Ask them before they arrive if there is anything specific they would like to do, then make plans accordingly. Often historic homes, museums, or places of interest have organized fundraisers during holiday or special event time. You and your guests might attend one or more of these.

These events take months of preparation. Knowledge of how to acquire all of these services, tickets and such are above and beyond what the average secretary or in-house coordinator needs to know to perform the duties for which they are paid. This is truly a time to call in a professional management event team.

CASE STUDY XIV

An association's annual meeting was held as a Christmas event. The association committee agreed that they wanted a professionally managed event, to enhance their reputation for superior quality.

The first step was to plan a theme that would encourage the membership to attend. The event had to be very promising, as there was so much demand on everyone's time during the month of December. The selected theme was "The Magic of the Season."

The logo and the design used on the invitation and other promotional pieces was a top hat with a sprig of holly in the hat band; a rabbit with a Christmas bell around its neck was peeking out of the hat. This invitation was designed using simple clip art and a high quality quick print shop.

A site, the ballroom of a local hotel, was selected for its size, ambience and convenient location.

A selection was made from the banquet menu. In addition, the seating and serving arrangements were discussed with the catering director.

The main event was a dance that followed a cocktail party and dinner. A local disc jockey played the groups favorite tunes, while making the entertainment more affordable. A magician was included for additional fun.

The centerpieces on the tables included items associated with magic, a sprig of holly and candles.

Some events need to be more conservative because of budgetary constraints. This is a fact of life — and there are lots of ways to overcome a frugal budget. Wise research and shopping can produce a fun-filled and effective event. The key ingredient is creativity!

CASE STUDY XV

Clients begin to look foward to annual events after a few years of repeat invitations and good times. This is a wonderful way to say "Thank you for your business," "Let's get to know each other better" or "Come see our new facility or equipment."

The key to success on repeated events is creativity! It carries the promise of surprise to your guests and builds your image. It implies you are innovative, quality oriented, caring of their opinions and "state-of-the-art." These are the main reasons you have special events.

Begin by getting your strongest creative minds together, or call a professional event management firm, and follow the steps set out in Chapter 3.

Some examples of some very successful annual holiday open houses follow:

Our client was a manufacturing company that had just added 30,000 square feet of warehouse space. They wanted to let their customers know of this new capability. An additional goal was the communication that with this new space they would control their industry in the future.

Our decorator was able to take advantage of this huge empty space, which offered 25-foot ceilings. It was a professional event decorator's dream.

Our theme was "Futuristic Holiday Fantasia." This combination of words was created to develop the desire to attend the event through mental pictures and promises.

The invitations were designed to bring the recipients emotional association of Christmas together with a high tech attitude. Thus, a contemporary silver mylar tree with geometric trimmings and surroundings was printed on high gloss neon paper, and sent to the clients guests list.

To maximize our budget, we chose to concentrate on one very large focal point and to surround it with food tables for the hors d'oeuvres. This was a statement of strength and professionalism. A

20-foot live pine tree was placed in the center of the hospitality area with a geometric 3-foot lighted star on the top. Hundreds of white twinkle lights were hidden in the branches, creating mystique. Clusters of silver and gold mylar ribbons, neon colored geometric ornaments and mirrored plexiglass rods were hung in appropriately pleasing places about the tree. Beveled mirror shapes further enhanced the theme and decor.

The tables were built to create a large circle around the tree when connected. The table top was silver mylar, which would both visually enlarge the table and food presentation and enhance any colorful food selections. The skirting was neon mylar in 1/4 inch strips, which created movement and good draping.

We provided attractive silver and mylar pieces to the caterer to incorporate into their tray presentations. In addition, neon was used as the accent colors in the contemporary table centerpieces.

The selected caterer worked hard to come up with foods of the future that would still appeal to the taste of todays' guests. We also created suggestive names, such as "Space Balls," and had them printed on small cards to describe the food and further strengthen our theme.

The servers were dressed in silver suits-of-tomorrow, accented in silver and neon holiday trim. They carried champagne and fine hors d'oeuvres on silver trays among the guests.

Background music was presented both live and taped through electronics. A special approach to combine traditional holiday music with high tech sounds was developed and played in rotation with two live synchronized electronic keyboards. This combination was a great crowd pleaser and also gave us what we needed for our presentation and the grand finale.

A record number of guests responded to our client's invitation, and, therefore, heard the verbal message about the company's past, present and future growth. They toured the new facility and this accomplished part of our goal. We still needed to solidify the memory and give these guests a reason to talk about the event, our client, and the company's capabilities.

The memory was created through state-of-the-art technology. As the president was closing with his appreciation for coming, the "2001" holiday music theme began to swell (this was especially created for this event). Colored smoke began to appear at the base of the Christmas tree and spread into the room with the little lights continuing to twinkle through the haze. Suddenly sharp, brilliant beams of laser lights pierced the foggy room, hitting the mirrors on the tree, bouncing back and forth about the room, in synchronization to the exciting music.

The surprise of hi-tech lasers created amazement and delight for the guests! They were further amazed at the additional sight of pyrotechnics shooting cold spark fountains at the base of the huge tree.

When the music and excitement was over, the guests left full of appreciation for such a fine evening. By association, they knew the business they would do with our client would have that same state-of-the-art quality. For that reason alone, we considered the event very successful.

CASE STUDY XVI

A medium sized company held an open house at Christmas time each year to entertain their clients. The goal was to communicate with existing customers, invite potential clients, and encourage more sales.

The theme was "A World of Thanks." It was a very direct message of appreciation for both the past year's business and the anticipated continuing relationship.

"Thanks" was creatively scripted in many languages, to be used on signage and decorative cards. The room was a blend of ethnic holiday decor, with costumed mannequins, lots of colors and twinkling lights. Stations representing Mexico, England, France and Germany were decorated according to customs for their finest holiday food presentations.

The entertainment that followed the buffet dinner was a delightful program of international Santas. Each Santa told joyful stories of the interesting traditions of their country's holiday celebrations.

We engaged a very versatile band which got into the spirit of the theme and played "sets" of music from four countries. They even changed their jackets and hats during intermissions to relate to the festive costumes of the countries they were representing. The guests seemed to appreciate their effort, and the combination of all their enthusiasms produced an outstanding, fun-filled evening.

Gifts from many nations were given to everyone from the different Santas. The guests, client, vendors and our Master of Ceremonies staff all went home with an increased international vocabulary, knowledge of international traditions and new appreciation for our client's business attitudes. This was one of those events that produced a real "emotional high" . . . everything was great!

CASE STUDY XVII

Our client had three areas of concern: the company holiday event had become a "dreaded drag"; there had been too much drinking; and the "camaraderie" had gotten out of hand, creating office romances. The company president was going to eliminate the annual office Christmas party.

The solutions we offered gave him the confidence to "try again" and treat his staff with a holiday event.

The first thing we did was select a unique facility, giving the guests a bit of curiosity and desire to attend. It was centrally located, close to town where their offices were, and had plenty of free parking.

We created a clever theme and announced it in a printed invitation sent to their homes. This suggested a special evening, especially developed for their enjoyment. The difference between the invitation and an office memo told them something special was in store.

The entertainment for the evening was selected to create a holiday mood — madrigal singers in costumes. In addition, a band played lively music — fun and fast dancing songs. Very few slow tunes were played to eliminate any suggestion of romance.

The decorations were extensive and beautiful. We had a huge table (10 feet x 10 feet) for the food and focal point, on which we created an ice skating pond. Snow banks and small sparkling snow covered trees were placed at the edges of silver mylar reflective sheets, representing ice. Clear twinkle lights laced and highlighted the scene, creating an icy shimmer. Charming animated figures in costumes skated gaily about the ice.

The food was placed at the edges of the scene on the white linen covered and skirted tables.

The table centerpieces were old fashioned wicker sleighs filled with charming Santas, gifts and snow covered pine cones. Red and green candles with ribbon accents were added and all were resting on 19" mirror rounds that carried this holiday festive glow about the room.

This extensive approach to decor again told the employees that management had gone to extra effort and expense to make this event special for them. This creates obvious employee good will.

The food menu was developed to appeal to the guests taste and go beyond their expectations.

The alcohol was controlled in several ways:

— Projection of a classy and professional atmosphere
— Bartender's control through observation of guests
— Drink tickets distributed upon arrival
— Plenty of food, soft drinks, punch and coffee
— The bar closed one hour before the end of the event

The guests all received a special tree ornament with the company logo and the year. This established a tradition to look forward to annually, as well as pride in employment longevity.

The C.E.O. of the company encouraged the light-hearted attitude of the group by being in the middle of the action. He set an example of how to play as he probably does on a daily basis of how to work.

The guests thoroughly enjoyed themselves. They ate a lot, danced a lot, talked and laughed, and 99% stayed until the very end.

The boss was pleased, as he said his final farewell, "Merry Christmas to all and to all a Good Night!"

By the way, we just finished coordinating our sixth Christmas event for this company. We are very proud of this success.

CASE STUDY XVIII

In an effort to show its appreciation, the management of a large corporation held a Christmas party with the theme, "Teaming Around the Tree." A special tune, sung to the melody of a familiar Christmas carol, was used as the invitation. It, too, emphasized teamwork. A large Christmas tree was the main focal point of the event. It was decorated with paper doll chains, again reflecting the idea of teamwork. Good food and drink was served to the fun music of a jug band.

Surrender to the charm of a "Good Ol' Country Christmas." A 20-foot fir tree laden with home-made ornaments, colorful beading and beautifully wrapped packages produces an enchanted scene. (Photography courtesy of Joe Prestigiacomo)

CASE STUDY XIX

There are a few community events that are so big that they are treated as "holidays." Corporations routinely participate in them, and use them for promotional and customer-relations purposes.

One of the biggest and most famous is held right here in my home town of Louisville, Kentucky — The Kentucky Derby Festival.

On Derby Day, International Aviation Company, whose clients are large corporations, entertains the pilots of the many corporate airplanes that have flown into Louisville for the Derby festivities. The business purpose is to provide the opportunity to refuel the planes, and, secondly, to accustom the pilots to flying into their facility on a routine basis.

This event originally started with the airport management providing grilled hamburgers for the pilots who were confined to the airport while their passengers were at the Derby.

After two years, management realized that entertaining the pilots was good public relations, and it was decided to expand the festivities by hiring a special events firm. The third year, 300 pilots attended the event from 9:30 a.m. to 6:00 p.m. The objective was to entertain as many pilots as possible in a positive and memorable manner. The theme was: "We're lucky in Kentucky to Host the Pilots That Are *Planely* the Best."

The hanger of the air terminal was decorated by covering the ceilings with elaborate kites of all sizes and brilliant colors. They were also used in the large tent which was located out on the lawn for the picnic. Traditional Kentucky food and drinks were served, although the mint juleps were actually non-alcoholic, and were called "Plane Juleps." The centerpiece reflected the logo — an airplane flying through a horseshoe. Activities such as horseshoe pitching, kite flying, and bubble blowing contests with prizes were held out on the lawn. Several televisions were placed behind the tent so people could watch the races at Churchill Downs.

After lunch, there were more activities in the hanger — musical entertainment, betting on the races with play money and an area set theatre-style, with a 12-foot television screen. Kentucky Derby Pie, ice cream from a machine, and lemonade were all available. Immediately before the final race, there was an auction held with a real auctioneer offering gifts of interest that could be bought with the play money accumulated during the day.

Southern hospitality abounds during the Kentucky Derby activities! Colorful striped tents, crisp white table linens and, of course, beautifully dressed belles add to the festive atmosphere.

This has been such a positive event that it has grown considerably over the years. More recently, the hanger was decorated to look like a miniature Churchill Downs with a tulip garden, a large tote board, a starting gate for the horses, and betting windows selling and paying off bets with play money. In addition, several companies set up table-top booths in the "paddock," which was a source of income to the host company. For people walking from the planes to the terminal, there was a red carpet with southern belles in antebellum dresses to personally greet them, and a costumed banjo player completing the picture of southern hospitality.

International Aviation Company recognizes this event to be a real public relations "bonanza." The pilots talked about the fun they had when they came to this airport to other pilots, as they flew around the country. This encouraged other pilots to fly into IAC not only for Derby, but at other times of the year.

CASE STUDY XX

A national hospital chain which combined its Grand Opening and Kentucky Derby entertaining made a very intelligent move. By combining the two events, it was able to bring people from all over the country to see this new representation of progress — its new health care facility. Immediately following, company officers took their guests, full of anticipation, to the Kentucky Derby.

Many influential people such as movie stars and dignitaries attended this event, knowing the Kentucky Derby would be added to their agenda. This important guest list gave greater credibility to the overall image of the corporation, the blessing of its future and, of course, the media enhancement was incomparable.

The media that attends the Kentucky Derby is not only numerous but also very prestigious. When they have the opportunity to cover something else of national interest during the same time span, this is (and was) a great advantage to both the media and the corporation.

The grand opening was on the wire service because of the people in attendance. This is an accomplishment that is the goal of every public relations professional. It is difficult to say how great the rewards or the return will be by having these people and this kind of media attention for a national company's grand opening. But we can certainly be sure it was worth every penny that was spent by the corporation.

In addition, this was a very elegant event, so the image that was projected was one of very high profile. Kentucky traditions dictated the concept used: the ultimate in Southern hospitality.

Depending on the atmosphere that is developed, sometimes a variety of music from Kentucky Bluegrass to classical may be appropriate. In this particular case, we used Kentucky Bluegrass at the entrance. It was lively, and built excitment and anticipation of a good time. Inside the facility we used a piano and in the tent we had a classical guitarist.

A very special touch was created for the event: we had a mint julep fountain instead of a champagne fountain. We had juleps flowing, totally surrounded by strawberries and mint. The silver julep cups, filled with crushed ice and mint, were placed around the fountain on silver trays where they could be filled by the guests.

Having the proper recipe for a Mint Julep is important — and since it is representative of part of the southern traditions, we take no chances. Master of Ceremonies has its own julep syrup and we provide it at Derby functions as part of our guaranteed service! The recipe was developed by my husband over the past twenty years. It is so sublimely delicious that a mere sip transforms you to a "southern" state-of-mind!

Realizing that some of the celebrities would not want to tour an entire facility, guests were allowed and encouraged to tour parts of the facility, roam the grounds and gracious gardens, and then return to the tent for food and drink. They were exposed to a sampling of what was important to the hospital, but the advantage of this kind of event was the mingling and the networking. The guests rubbing elbows with "special people," and the ability to say they stood beside Zsa Zsa Gabor at the hospital grand opening was very good for public relations.

The theme of the event was "A Real Kentucky Thoroughbred — It's A Sure Bet." That implied to the invitees that the event would definitely have the Kentucky Derby atmosphere, it would be a lot of fun and was worth their attendance. When they left, they carried in their minds the message of our client — "This, indeed, is one of Kentucky's newest and finest hospitals, and the investments this organization is planning in cities around the country will all be of high quality." The company is still reaping public relations benefits from this event and it occured *seven* years ago.

Chapter
14

Picnics

CHAPTER 14

PICNICS
Organizing Folks, Food and Fun — No Matter What!

Corporations, small businesses and associations have Picnics. The purpose of such an event for a company is motivation for the employees to work well together, to generate more business if possible, and to foster general goodwill. This is a team-building effort that creates good feelings. For associations, the goals might be to entertain the existing members and solicit new memberships.

The planning steps are the same as previously discussed for other events in Chapter 3. It can be done by members of different departments, or, in the case of associations, by an appointed committee. Of course, a special events coordinator can contribute special industry knowledge such as available facilities, risk management and entertainment options.

The first thing to consider is the facility, which must be easily accessible to all the employees/members. A call to your local and state parks departments will get you a list of surrounding parks and what they offer. Be aware of their established rules and hours.

Obviously, the appropriate time is when the weather will be moderate. However, tents or pavillions need to be serious considerations because of bad weather. Tents also add a special attitude to picnics. They seem to say "management cared enough to get you the very best!"

By establishing the time in the late afternoon, only one meal must be served, and families can usually attend. People especially like to meet fellow employees' children and spouses.

The most frequent (and I'll add intelligent) food choice is traditional picnic fare such as hamburgers, chicken, or hot dogs cooked on a grill; salads (always keeping in mind the risk of spoilage); baked beans, etc. Food can be provided by a caterer, paid for by management, or everyone can participate by bringing pot luck dishes. An ice cream machine is always fun for everyone. They can be rented and operated by committee members. Other suggestions are, cotton candy, snow cones and lemonade shake-ups, all of which make for a carnival and fun-filled atmosphere.

Sports-related games are fun and fitting at picnics. Sack races, baseball, spoon relays, and dunking booths are popular (particularly when managers are in the dunking booth). Other group activities include sing-alongs, lawn croquet, tug-of-war, football, and card games for those who are less active. It is also fun to provide a singing group to entertain; and, for the children, clowns who make balloon sculptures or storytellers are popular.

Because attendance at these events can sometimes be disappointing, the promotion must be enthusiastic and strong. If management talks about the up-coming day with a spirited attitude, it is helpful. Banners placed around the workplace can also engender the desire to attend, along with festive invitations which could include a balloon printed with the time, date, and location to give to the children so they will be aware of the picnic and encourage the parents to attend.

A theme for your picnic will help excite your guests. It describes what to expect at the event and subliminally states that you have gone the extra length to make their day special.

In addition, a theme will give you a point of departure for decorations and entertainment.

A few suggestions for picnic themes are:

Musical
"In the Good Ol' Summertime"
"Meet Me In St. Louis"
"State Fair"
"Take Me Out to the Ball Game"

TV Shows
"It's A Charlie Brown Picnic"
"The (Company Name) Family Picnic"

Play Time
> "All Work and No Play Makes Work Dull . . ."
> "Camp (Company Name)"
> "Family Recognition Day"
> "Family-Fun-Food Festival"
> "Teaming Up"
> "The (Company Name) Bash/Ball/Balloons/
>   Burger and Beer Day"

A professionally managed event allows all of your employees to participate, giving those who traditionally have "gotten stuck" with this monumental task the ability to enjoy the day and feel appreciated as well.

When combined with special touches that say "We care and appreciate you and your efforts," the annual picnic can effectively produce a sound return on the investment.

Nostalgic ideas of the "good old days," along with food, games and camaraderie, produce positive responses to attend the annual company picnic. It is fun for all!

Chapter
15

Parades

CHAPTER 15

PARADES
Procedures to Produce Moving Colors

"I love a parade." Who doesn't? Corporate and association parade participation can equal positive exposure if all of the circumstances are right. That is, if your organization fits the theme and mood of the parade and its sponsors; if it's in your market; and if the parade is the right level of quality for you.

Parades have been around for decades and, because of their acceptance and popularity, are a part of our social and promotional lives. While standing in the heat of summer or cold of winter, the parade watchers are unaware, in most cases, that they are watching fancy advertisements! Every single float is selling something. It could be the Boy Scouts, Girl Scouts or Brownies selling memberships through recognition and awareness, or a large appliance company selling its name and product.

Avon Cosmetics is a believer in this special event medium. They routinely enter parades and often win top prizes for their floats. It is a sure thing to say they also get top exposure from this medium. They feel the Tournament of Roses Parade, for example, is tailor-made for Avon's objectives. It is the perfect fit for their wholesome, clean-cut image.

1979 was Avon's debut in the nationally recognized parade, which was themed "Our Wonderful World of Sports." They entered a float featuring six female sports champions. Each athlete was interviewed separately by the press corps and two of them were on network telecasts.

Foreign press receptions were held before the parade in Pasadena, California for international relations. Avon has become the exclusive beauty consultant to the Rose Queen and her court, and hosts beauty seminars using this title. They use their sales brochures and publications to promote the Rose parade and their connection to such a successful and widely-known event.

The Pasadena Tournament of Roses Association has facts to prove its parade is "the world's greatest advertising bargain." Over 100 million people see the Rose Parade on network TV, via newspaper articles, souvenir magazines, plus an on-site audience of two million.

Not all parades command this kind of attention, but many of them are regionally important and professionally attractive.

Organizing a parade is definitely not for amateurs — other than the neighborhood Fourth of July parade of dressed-up dogs, colorful bikes, and children with triangular newspaper hats. Not that that kind of parade is less special — it is certainly close to my heart, but it is not a professional endeavor.

If an organization is investing promotionally budgeted funds in this medium, it must realize a public relations return. The parade must project the right image. It must be run professionally and have been promoted adequately. It must deliver a specific message to a targeted market on the sides of the street or to those watching on TV.

Parades require so much organization that they most often are done by teams of volunteers, or parade specialists. Promotion of the event is monumental and publicity should be just as extensive to get people to the parade. The organization is by no means simple. There are parade permits, finding facilities large enough to build floats, fire considerations, vendor permits, assisting and ultimately pleasing the participants in the parade and praying weather-related prayers!

Having established this viability, our next consideration will be questions of company involvement. Questions such as:

— Is a parade a good investment for you?
— *Which* parade is best?
— Can you promote your organization within this parade's theme?
— The float — buy or build?
— If you chose to build, will it be by professionals or company volunteers?
— *Timing* for *your* organization
— Insurance considerations

A facility for building the float is necessary, because many corporations have no manufacturing plants. The door size of the facility should be checked for height and width, to be sure the built float can be removed. It must also have power, water and good security.

Float beds vary — they can be made from automobile or house trailer frames, farm wagons, or can be specially built. The pulling unit, which has to move at about 2 1/2 miles per hour, most often is a tractor, but can be a truck, car, forklift, or something built to work within the design of the whole unit. The parade organizers are particular about the pulling element, because if the float breaks down, the parade stops.

Dimensions of a float unit are *usually* between 35 feet and 65 feet in length, 13 feet high for traveling, but can be extended when reaching the parade starting point. Width of the float for travel can be up to 8 feet for legal highway requirements and for display extended to 30 feet. (These are general rules and will vary with parades and their routes and needs.) The size of the float will ultimately be determined by the parade route for which it is built. Look for bridge heights, cross wires, the turning radius of tight corners and dips in the road. Artistic concerns will then be the final factors determining its size.

Signage is usually acceptable, but commercial messages are most often eliminated by the parade supervisory committee.

The parade committee will necessarily be the governing body of such an event, enforcing safety and other rules for the benefit of everyone involved. An open relationship will be advantageous to an organization planning a float.

Be prepared to present written copy describing your float to parade officials and the press. This will enhance your possibilities of getting coverage and having the message told the way you want it told.

Your creative team will brainstorm to develop the best approach for your float. You will then call in a professional float designer to help design and mechanically produce the float structure and decorations. The committee will have plenty of responsibilities, even with the professionals, who give them direction. Only quality materials should be used, since this is an image enterprise and safety considerations are involved.

The float builder will provide the committee with a scale model and a blueprint before beginning the project. Altogether, the work will take approximately 3 1/2 months.

Check with your insurance agency to be sure you have the necessary coverage for this undertaking. The float committee will expect this information early in the planning stage.

Most parades have prizes to motivate the participants to build quality floats. Winning such a prize will extend the perceived value of your promotional investment, with newspaper and television coverage reinforcing the company name.

When the parade is over, the float will go back to the warehouse, and everyone will be pleased with the entire project when the realization hits them — "What do we do with this monster now?" My philosophy is *save it* — you never know when you may need it! There are always other parades in which you could be involved. This will double the return on your investment — and that's always good!

Chapter
16

Festivals

—

CHAPTER 16

FESTIVALS
Managing Multitudinous Merrymaking

For those who have to organize them, festivals mean "mega-details." They take months to plan and organize, hundreds of people to coordinate, and are almost totally at the mercy of the weather. Let one detail slip through the cracks and it taints the entire festival with that ugly word — "unorganized."

For such a tremendous effort, one should look for a festival management firm. Not just because it is a lot of work, but also because your image is very vulnerable with a festival. A professional events producer will need to rely on volunteers for the massive manpower needed, so your organization will still be very involved. However, if you must do the job with a management staff "in-house," you need to search for experience in your key people.

Festivals usually begin with a committee. The committee has an objective: to raise money, celebrate something, or build community awareness. The basic rules for direction apply, plus some additional considerations. Let's review them quickly:

— Determine your goals
— How much money do you need to raise?
— How many people do you need to draw?
— What kind of publicity are you after?
— How best can you accomplish these goals?
— Do you have the budget to produce this event?
— Do you have the manpower necessary?
— What are your long-range goals for this festival and can the future of your organization support these goals?
— What kind of festival is best for your needs?

— Where can this event be held — consider the audience's convenience, electricity capabilities, size, parking, lighting, drainage. Is it a desirable location, one that will motivate attendance?

— Who will support this undertaking? You will need financial assistance, media cooperation, and your organization's total commitment.

— When will this festival be best attended? How long will it take to produce it comfortably? And what is your competition for attendance at that time? Weather is naturally your biggest consideration.

— Where can you get the elements you need for your event, such as games, prizes, props, entertainment?

— What are your risks? Be *very thorough* because of your legal liability.

After sorting through the previous considerations and making some decisions, you are ready to begin festival planning. Pull together your " team" to get your festival created, organized and executed. Your person in charge needs to be just that — in charge and experienced. In the beginning, get all the people you can. The good ones will shine, so you'll know who to pick for your committee heads. Then create an outline of committees by need and write job descriptions.

Select your theme. The theme will tell your audience what to expect at the festival. For maximum attendance you will want to come up with something that has worked before for others — but definitely try to make it new, fresh and creative.

Develop a budget according to need, then add other things you want. You will want to balance your expected revenue with anticipated expenses, keeping your sights on your goal. And be aware that most expenses will need to be paid *before* you produce any money. Some of the expenses you can anticipate for a festival are: publicity, entertainment, printing and postage, site fees, rental fees, tents, booths, tables and chairs, stages, sound systems, security, electrical power, labor fees, food and beverage, prizes, decorations, licenses and permits, insurance and management fees.

Check the community calendar and decide on your date. Will

it be a single day or multiple days? Does it conflict with any other events?

Publicity is next — it can mean success if handled properly. Paid media advertising to your audience is a big expense. Perhaps there are less expensive ways to get the word out — direct mail, posters, hand bills, bumper stickers and printed invitations, are all considerations. Public relations efforts —press releases and phone calls — will also contribute. Appearances on TV talk shows or radio programs by your festival coordinators will be very advantageous.

Celebrities also bring out people — by announcing their participation, you are automatically advertising the festival.

Seek corporate sponsorship if necessary. This is most successfully accomplished when the sponsor's product and the festival theme complement each other.

The design of the layout of the event will reflect the professionalism of the festival. It requires thoroughly thinking through the event from various perspectives.

Design the stage and its background as your focal point. Put your theme and colors on signage to remind people of your message. Continue using these colors in your other displays, booths and entrance areas.

Your walkways will be designed to accomodate your anticipated crowd, but, in general, allow at least eight people in width.

Signage can be decorative as well as functional. It should include the schedule of events, areas for food, restrooms and first aid. If this is a large festival, it would be good to have a map on a sign near the entrance.

If you have special attractions for children, you will want to scale down everything in their area to their size.

Look for wires, ropes, holes and tent pegs. Those you cannot repair or change need to be marked to avoid accidents.

Food and beverage stands, as well as places to eat, are best placed throughout the grounds for accessibility and to keep the traffic flowing.

Booths and Rides

Renting equipment, such as booths and tents, is far more cost-effective in the first year of your festival than purchasing them. If your event becomes successful, then you can think of buying equipment. When you do, the next consideration is storage of these large items.

The yellow pages of your telephone directory will direct you to tent rentals, booths, tables and chairs. There are supply companies, novelty stores, paper supply houses and concessions listed to help with your needs.

"Themed" festivals will dictate "themed" materials and will set the expectations of your attendees. International events, for example, will feature lots of food concessions, some clothing, jewelry, crafts, and books. The biggest setting you will create is the entertainment area — usually a stage, a backdrop, and a seating area in front.

Some festivals will have rides. You must check with local governmental agencies for their rules and permits. In summer months rides are in great demand because of fairs and carnivals. This should be considered during your date selection process. You may want to bring in only children's rides because of cost and liability associated with more elaborate set-ups.

Rides add excitement and motivate attendance. You cannot depend on them for revenue however, because you will have to guarantee the owners of the equipment a predetermined amount of money plus a percentage of tickets sold.

People love to eat and that is part of the draw to any festival. High-quality standards in the food concessions are a must for your success in the short and long terms. Obviously, you must be aware of and abide by the local health board rules.

Entertainment, specifically music, is perhaps the main reason people attend festivals. Jazz, rock-n-roll, country, whatever the style, there are plenty of fans for each, enough to build an entire weekend of celebrations.

Local entertainers are less costly, but the big names will draw the crowds. And this is generally when you start looking for a sponsor. Talent resources are listed in your yellow pages under — TALENT! These talent agencies are professionals and have first-hand experience

with today's performers. They know how to negotiate contracts —
which can be tricky — and they understand light and sound requirements. This must not be underestimated — both light and sound are big
issues for top artists. High voltage is a must and it is costly. Top groups
will demand proper dressing facilities and refreshments. It will be in
the contract. Read your contracts very carefully!

Other considerations for your festival:

— Are there permits required?
— Crowd control
— Parking attendance with good plans, identification and
   communication systems
— First aid station and medical professionals
— Portable toilets
— Clean-up crews
— Bookkeeping and banking
— Fire prevention
— Electrical safety considerations
— Uniforms for identification by attendees
— Legal needs — such as contracts
— Insurance and liability
— and much more!

There are many areas of responsibility in festival production. It
is an undertaking few people will attempt without great resources.
Therefore, we suggest you absorb what you have read and consider
how much work it entails. If you want to produce a festival, look for
detailed "how-to" information from experienced festival producers or
ask them to assist you through consultation. It is the intelligent thing
to do, and your festival will be far greater for your good judgment.

Chapter
17

Sponsorships

CHAPTER 17

SPONSORSHIPS
Creating "Win-Win" Promotional Investments

The subject of event corporate sponsorship is so exciting! It is a special form of advertising that benefits the two involved parties equally in most cases. Seldom do you see such a "win-win" situation.

Event sponsorships usually work this way: corporations are called upon by organizations to underwrite all or part of a special event. This event can be large or small, but the important considerations for the corporation are that the event be worthy of community support and that the attendees are consumers of the sponsor's product or service. An example is a tennis tournament sponsored by, say, Wilson tennis equipment. The name "Wilson" will be on printed pieces, signage, in the name of the tournament and in any media coverage, just to mention a few possibilities.

Corporate sponsorships arose as a good way — sometimes the only way — to finance big community events. Generally no event will produce enough money through ticket sales alone to produce the quality event that is expected by the community, and still leave enough money to benefit the sponsor.

Sponsorship of events evolved from the tradition of philanthropy, one of the oldest forms of corporate social responsibility. Companies build stronger communities in which they can thrive, while polishing their image, by giving dollars to worthy causes.

Times have changed the way businesses view their methods of charitable giving. Everything has become more bottom line oriented. Corporations still want the public relations benefits of community donations, but they want to see greater returns on those investments.

The potential public relations benefits of sponsoring the "right event" by a corporation is immense. It is obvious that visibility is the greatest reason for investing — so research is essential in deciding what event to support. There are basic questions to be answered: What is the maximum market exposure? How many customers can be reached? What are the expenses involved? Can a return on investment be calculated?

Corporations are realizing that event sponsorship can positively affect the bottom line, if targeted wisely as part of their marketing plan. How does it help? In many ways:

Better Brand Identification — "Events identify a brand's image, they give it personality in a more tangible way than can media advertising," says an Anheuser-Busch manager. The company's sponsorship of triathlon competitions or powerboat racing tells consumers that the brand is the appropriate choice for those who enjoy participating in or watching those sports.

More Focused Marketing — "Event sponsorship can deliver a targeted group of customers and represent a brand as an appropriate, related choice for their interests," says another beer industry spokesman. That is perhaps why super premium Lowenbrau beer sponsors a Porsche 962 on the prestigious International Motor Sports Association circuit, while Miller's popularly priced Meister Brau brand sponsors truck and tractor-pull competitions.

A Friend-in-the-Community Positioning — By sponsoring events of local interest, a corporation can reap the public relations benefit of positioning itself as not only a good neighbor, but also a provider and preserver of "good things" in the community.

Promoting Cities

City-sponsored festivals are great vehicles for promoting the urban sections of cities. Formerly barren streets can bustle with activities, restaurants and shops can open their doors and tourists will gather when there is a quality city festival going on.

Towns like Norfolk and San Antonio have made special events, and the resulting tourism, big business. Baltimore today has earned strong national awareness through city government's efforts to bring people downtown. Thousands of events create 22,000 jobs and sell 3,000 hotel rooms there.

Louisville, Kentucky, has built an entire city festival out of the running of the Kentucky Derby. The race is two minutes long, but the special events stretch out for at least two weeks. The Kentucky Derby Festival is now world-renowned as one of the largest and most successful city festivals. The possibilities for exposure at these events can also be world wide, through television and other media coverage. For corporate sponsors, that adds up to very valuable corporate visibility.

Shopping Malls

Shopping malls, the new "Main Streets" of America, sponsor events to promote their stores and bring large numbers of people into a shopping environment.

They have developed special events departments to augment their marketing and advertising efforts.

In some cases, the large mall management firms will move from city to city with packaged, sponsored events.

Examples of sponsored events would be fashion shows, musical groups of varying sizes and types, childrens contests, dance exhibitions, automobile and flower shows, health screenings and animal events.

Political Sponsors

Politics and special events go together naturally.

A wise aspiring politician will seek out and hire a very talented special event producer as part of his promotional team. For fundraisers, dinners, press conferences and hundreds of other kinds of public events, a special events planner with flair and experience can create just the right atmosphere and maximum effect.

Surveys and Statistics

According to a nationwide survey conducted by Philip Joel Shuman on successful sponsorships: 53% of consumers said they would buy from sponsoring companies. Figures climbed to 63% for skilled workers, 66% for age 50 and over and 73% for consumers in $20,000 to $30,000 income bracket (Special Events Report, October 13, 1986, Vol. 5, No. 20).

Most corporations who become involved in this form of promotion do so in a variety of categories rather than just one area: cultural events (57%), sport (54%), community (52%) and music (40%). Approximately 21% reported no sponsorships at all.

The average price of sponsorships will range from $500,000 for a national event to $5,000 for a local event.

The percentage of a participating company's advertising budget for sponsorhip is approximately 23% of their total marketing/communication outlay.

Objectives of sponsorships: community relations (24%), awareness (20%), image (15%), corporate responsibility (15%) and sales (9%). However, we all know that any company in business spends money to improve their bottom line; everything is sales related.

The survey stated future expenditures for sponsored events was "rosy!" Forty-nine percent of those who sponsor events will continue a significant outlay over the next three to five years. Twenty-five percent see a 10% increase, some a 25% increase; 3% said it would go up to 50%. Only 6% said it would decrease.

A survey was made of consumer response also, to see if a sponsorship had ever made an individual buy a sponsor's product. Community events scored (58%), music (48%), sports (41%). Macy's Thanksgiving Day Parade scored highest with a recall of 97%.

Olympic sponsorship retention is also high. Even after a year, 73% could name at least one official sponsor.

Pepsi's sponsorship of the Michael Jackson Victory Tour scored 56% retention and it was held in 1984, two years prior to this survey.

The twenty-one to thirty-six year old age group scored highest in associating an event with its sponsor, except for the cultural events. The fifty-plus age group ranked highest there.

Income levels of best retentions was $50,000 plus, with professional people leading those tested.

Fifty-three percent (53%) felt "more likely to buy" the sponsor's product after having attended their event.

Cultural institutions report that corporations provided an average of 23% of their special events budget and 10% of their operating budgets.

The typical value of a corporate contribution was $4,703. For large special events the average was $104,643.

All in all, this hands-on form of communication, if done well, will bring together buyers and sellers in a positive and memorable way, proving again that the special event is an effective marketing tool.

Chapter
18

Corporate
Theater

CHAPTER 18

CORPORATE THEATRE
The Dramatic Power of Persuasion

Corporate theatre involves the use of actors (professional or amateur) to dramatize a company's image, a new product, or the history of an organization. Anything is possible, from dancing vegetables to a rock-n-roll show. Perhaps a circus with elephants, a rodeo, a special song with lyrics, or a chorus line are appropriate for promotional purposes. Any of these kinds of show-stoppers can be incorporated into a company's meeting to give it sparkle and create a positive memory.

Performances by costumed characters creatively and effectively relay high-impact messages, corporate techniques, policies or programs.

An important message will be remembered when presented through business theatre. For example, I have seen our leading soft drink companies, Pepsi and Coke, introduce new products in a stage production with dancers wearing aluminum cans and dancing to the new theme song. That was a memorable way to make a strong first impression of the new soft drink.

A corporate production can also be *fun*. It can be personalized by mentioning specific employees' names — something everyone likes. With the right combination of fun and message, a theatrical production can motivate and change attitudes.

Business meetings and anniversary celebrations are a good

time to use this creative approach. For corporate birthdays, a history of the company, presented in the form of a play or skit, can create a sense of pride, accomplishment, understanding and loyalty.

I particularly enjoy this promotional capability because I have seen how successful it can be. When done well, a point can be made and retained by the targeted audience. In addition, I must have a bit of "show biz" in my blood. Even though our company develops the concept, hires the actors through auditions, writes the scripts, determines the set design and costuming and directs the production, I am always thrilled to tears and cheers at the final scene, as if I were a spectator for the first time. A few case studies follow to give you examples of effective corporate theatre.

CASE STUDY XXI

"Einstein Promotes Polymers"

To culminate a very successful Grand Opening for a polymers company we wanted a punch of pizzazz! Our goal was to surprise our sophisticated audience and send them out into the business community discussing what they had experienced with people who would be touched indirectly by the event and gain awareness of our client.

The theme for the event was a take-off of their molecule logo, "Molecular Momentum." This molecule had been reproduced in several ways for the event — the printed invitation, a 12-foot mylar balloon sculpture for the front of the building, the centerpieces and a

A "scientist", surrounded by smoke, and still holding a beaker of experimental solution, touts the qualities of our fine client — in a credible manner.

crystal gift. To continue this theme, we developed a short production for the finale at the sit-down luncheon.

The speeches were complete and the meal was almost over

when, suddenly, in an anteroom, an explosion was heard and smoke began to pour from under the door. The door burst open and there, in a cloudy haze, stood a befuddled scientist with clothes and hair awry, a very confused expression on his face and holding a beaker of foaming green chemicals. With his thick German accent, he asked the crowd, "Where am I?" "Ah, yes," he says, "I'm at the ABC Polymers Company — the finest polymers plant in all of the world ... " and on he went, touting the merits of our client. Therein lies the power of corporate theatre — someone else delivers a company's message, making it more credible than if the company said it themselves.

People of all walks of life and sophistication become very involved in these short productions — partly out of the surprise when it happens. The scientist left the room as quickly as he appeared, I could hear people saying "Who was that?" "Where did he come from?" "Where did he go?" It was tremendous!

CASE STUDY XXII

P.T. Barnum Motivates the Sales Staff to Stay at the Big Top

A corporate sales meeting finale was designed to take place under a Big Top made of balloons and pennants in the corporate colors, in a hotel ballroom. The theme of the two day event was "At The Top," making reference to the company's position in the industry.

Decor, entertainment such as clowns, mimes, animal acts and circus music set the stage for the company's general manager, who was posing as the ring master. After giving out the annual awards, the music heightened, the spotlights began searching and criss-crossing as a highly polished and spirited P. T. Barnum enthusiastically appeared in the center ring dressed in sequins, high top hat and cutaway.

As the circus music culminated, P. T. Barnum's gloved hands, reached out to the audience and excitedly appealed:

"Ladies and Gentlemen — and children of all ages — and fellow showmen! What's that you say? Your're not showmen! Oh, but you are, everyone in sales is a showman!"

P. T. Barnum continued, making reference occasionally to an object in the next ring. A lovely circus lady, dressed in a colorful satin costume with fur and feathers, stood guard. He made this object magical with his words and contagious attitude. At just the right time, toward the end of this presentation, he asked the lady to remove the cover. The music and lights came up, the balloons flew to the tent top and there in the mystical dust remained an air compressor — the product they all sold daily! P. T. Barnum had put *magic* in the product and created a new sales attitude.

The audience of salesmen (showmen) all cheered and left with renewed motivation to sell. This was tremendously successful. The key is to assess needs and create productions to achieve goals.

Corporate theatre is an exciting and effective medium, but needs the creative guidance of a professional production team. Our firm created the theme, the production concept, the script, auditioned for the P. T. Barnum role, designed the set, the lighting, the music and directed all of these elements.

Chapter
19

Special
Effects

CHAPTER 19

SPECIAL EFFECTS
Imaginative Images

What a glorious and exciting time we are all privileged to live in! We are exposed to so many new and different technological innovations every time we turn on the television or go shopping at the grocery store.

This exposure is a subtle education into the world of special effects! Because of this continuing display, today's generation is fairly sophisticated in its taste for visual technology.

Event producers have the knowledge of special effects capabilities, the resources of professional talent to provide the services and the creative ambition to want to utilize special effects whenever possible.

Too often the ugly word "budget" enters the picture and limits the opportunity for special effects inclusion in many of our events. Time will be the answer to this situation, as it has always been with new and great things.

Special effects are created electrically and electronically with gases and gun powder, steam, chemicals, water, textures and film. Their transforming catalysts are fiber optics, pyrotechnics, dozens of forms of lighting, including laser lights of many types and intensities. Special effects include audio visuals projecting scenery to fireworks, slide productions, some with multi-screens and projections, and sound from various systems, including those created through a synthesizer. The new technology of environmental "soundscapes" is fascinating and effective.

Teleconferencing is quite an addition to some special productions. We recently created the celebration for the grand opening of the Telecommunications Research Center in Louisville, Kentucky, at which time a link to Germany demonstrated the potential for teleconferencing internationally. The presentation was made in a manner that utilized the equipment, and its product alone was the "special effect" of the evening — it was quite exciting!

Confetti cannons and streamer cannons create both sound and sight effects. These cannons can be rented at theatrical lighting stores, but must be very carefully handled. They use a small explosive cartridge to project the papers. You need either experience or very good instruction for the person igniting them. Mylar confetti is terrific, causing a twinkling effect as it lands. (Glitter can be loaded with this, too). Caution! Glitter can get into the eyes quite easily.

Safety should always be a major consideration in the use of special effects — they can touch your audience mentally *and* physically! Snow machines are wonderful for effects, for example,but the product is wet and could harm some clothing. Once we used a bubble machine in a trade show booth which created a wonderful fantasy effect for our client. However, the booth in back of his was serving chocolate covered strawberries — occasionally covered with bubble soap. You cannot control those "tiny bubbles!"

Balloons are lots of fun for developing an attitude — thus they are a good special effect. The tubular balloons can stretch for "rooms,"creating all kinds of mental images. They can also add lots of color.

Fog machines are an established fact of special effects life! Despite being used almost routinely for the theatre, fog can still turn heads when done well at special events. In the case study that follows, I'll describe how we used it with lights to promote a company's new capability. Fog must accompany many types of lighting, such as lasers, for the light rays to be seen. Fog can be produced from small spray cans to bulky barrels filled with dry ice, hoses, and a motor. We have used one of those old machines and now opt to go with the smaller machines that you plug in and control remotely.

Fiber optics are fascinating and their future is unlimited. The fiber optic screens can produce a wide range of illusions, from romance to space age wonder. Fiber optic centerpieces with battery power can create a special ambiance for a variety of themes.

Motorized stages, complete sets or single props that move in a scene are effects to be considered. The overall beauty and spectacle of an elaborate focal point we created for a grand opening was truly magnified when it was presented on a rotating round stage. The viewers were made aware, without words, that they were supposed to look at the whole piece! You might recall that is how car dealers proudly present their new models — the revolving stage, bright lights and beautiful people are all special effects, drawing the viewers' attention to the product.

Included in special effects can be fans to produce movement; slit curtains of mylar in many colors, creating swirling illusions; water; and textures that the audience must touch.

Oversized props can create oversized emotions. A gigantic, real looking, feeling and smelling chocolate truffle will produce a memory for a chocolate lover for a lifetime.

Computers are the back-stage geniuses of many of our special effects. They control the way our lasers dance from mirror to mirror or in various patterns. They coordinate sight and sound, such as fireworks shows to symphony music. Computers regulate fountains of water to dance to music, as well as change their colors.

Pyrotechnics are truly today's sizzle! Fireworks have been

Exhilarating, breathtaking, exciting . . . all accurately describe this grand opening ceremony. Pyrotechniques and a dramatic laser show heralded the completion of the airport terminal. (Photograph courtesy of Joe Eden Photography)

"bursting in air" and full of "red glare" for many fourth of Julys — and I personally hope this never grows old or commonplace. I love patriotism and whatever instills that emotion in all of us. But today, our "pyro-pros" can produce such wonderful effects for our events. Anyone who has seen the evening finale at Epcot Center can testify that the combination of lasers and fireworks is a truly spectatcular show.

In the grand opening case study of the airport I described the use of pyrotechniques. I was fascinated as I watched the experts climb out on the glass dome of the terminal rotunda to position the charges. They put cold spark fountain charges in the huge centerpiece, and in addition, there were rockets shooting across the room on wire tracks over the heads of the audience. All this was ignited simultaneously as a prelude to the laser show. The audience screamed with amazement and delight. It was explosive!

Laser lights create much the same excitement as fireworks and their penetrating beams of light can be used to produce many effects. The argon lasers are very intense and can project great distances. The exact distance is dependent on the technical components, which is determined by professional laser light experts. These lasers are great for large areas or outdoor community events. They are cooled with water and need to be kept over the heads of the crowd. Graphics, including logos, can be projected on a wall or screen, which can tell a story, or the reason for the celebration, or identify a sponsor.

Our company recently purchased two "Variscan" laser simulators to be used for corporate promotional events. They are high-intensity arc lamps, air cooled, can be plugged into 110 outlets and are of no danger to crowds. They are computer controlled and can produce pre-programmed designs to the beat of music. These lights are great for smaller settings — night clubs, hotel ballrooms and convention trade shows. The light is also beamed off strategically-positioned mirrors, and a less experienced technician can be utilized for their operation. Use of this equipment is a very good example of how technology produces lower prices and minimal operational needs for special effects. The future is truly so exciting!

Lighting is necessary and it is sometimes a luxury, but it can also provide total decor if handled correctly by an expert. We have used many types of lights for years — the tiny Italian lights, pinspots, strobes, black lights, beacons and rope lights. I love the effects created with gobo patterns affixed to lights that, when projected, produce trees, snowflakes or company logos.

Sound is a similar field that produces wonderful special effects. "Soundscapes" are compositions of sounds created to simulate various situations. A good example would be Paul Revere's ride during a rain storm. One hears his horse thundering over cobblestones, through fields of grass, puddles, over bridges and more. Romantic moods can be created with the sound of ocean waves, distant fog horns and cooing sea gulls. These sounds are most often produced with synthesizers, then mixed in sound studios by experienced technicians. Tapes of prerecorded sounds can also be used.

This book was written to be instructional. But when it comes to special effects, the advice I strongly give is to call a professional. This is an area of expertise that, in many cases, is dangerous. Special effects such as pyro, lasers, sound or hi-tech lighting take skill and knowledge. The pros are licensed, know their equipment and can produce your needs for special effects efficiently, successfully and, above all, safely. These experts can be found through the assistance of an event professional, preferably one who is a member of the International Special Events Society (ISES). Special effects technicians will be listed in their membership directory.

CASE STUDY XXIII

A printing company purchased an expensive and highly technical piece of printing equipment, giving them new and very broad capabilities. They wanted to get the word out to their clients, potential clients and the local business community for general image enhancement.

In addition, the company was celebrating a 50th anniversary, and wanted to use the opportunity to let its employees and their families share the excitement of this new acquisition.

The theme we selected"The Head Hantscho" was a take-off on the manufacturer's name of the new press — "Hantscho."

The invitation to the open house, in my opinion, was perfect! It was printed by the host company, giving guests a sample of the high quality of their work. We suggested the high-tech and future capabilities of the press by likening it to a space ship. The caption was "The Head Hantscho Has Landed in Louisville." We purchased the rights to a popular color photo of the city's skyline for the bottom of the 8 1/2" x 11" folded card.

When the invitation was opened, the new press was shown in its full color glory. Date, time and place were reversed out of the color. The piece was beautiful and of high quality, and served as a great printing sample, especially for those who could not attend the open house. Our designer did an excellent job on this invitation. My advice is to seek the best art talent you can afford, and work hard on developing a solid work relationship with that person. Remember, the end result

This invitation doubled as a promotion piece for the company's new capabilities.

of any phase of your event is only as good as your selected vendors.

Our client wanted to have two events, one in the evening for the V.I.P.s and customers and one for the employees on a Saturday afternoon.

Thursday evening was recommended. We have always found attendance best on that night of the week. A cocktail menu of hors d' oeuvres was beautifully presented around a color scheme of yellow, magenta, blue and black, which represented the four colors used in the printing process. Wine, beer, tea and soft drinks were served, as with many such events, minimizing the risk of too much alcohol.

Liquids need to be given extra consideration during extreme hot or cold times of the year. Your guests will expect hot coffee when they are cold and, as in this case, iced tea when they are hot.

The facility was cleaned and readied for its inspection — not always an easy task when a company has an older, very large building, plus a full daily schedule of work. This is something we stress with our clients up front. Our event team even goes through the building recommending areas to further clean if necessary — we can see what their guests will see, and we all want their image to be totally positive.

A large welcoming banner was hung on the exterior of the building, and as a further welcome, musicians were in the lobby as the guests entered.

After tours of the office and plant, the guests gathered for the ceremonial recognition of the new printing press. The lights went completely down, smoke filled the room and colored lights came up to highlight the 40-foot long press. Appropriate music helped set the mood. The owner of the company began his description of this machine. Suddenly, laser lights pierced the smoke to point a beam directly to the section of the press being described. Lasers from another direction danced about in various graphic designs intermittently to excite the audience and further state the high tech message being delivered. This program was only seven minutes long, however, I am sure the guests attention was total and the information absorbed.

Everyone enjoyed the client's hospitality and other guests, and our mission was accomplished in great style.

The employee event was also very enjoyable. The caterer cooked hamburgers, hot dogs and brats outside and filled out the meal with picnic foods and desserts. We set up tables in an empty area of the plant and covered them with plastic cloths in our event colors of blue, magenta and yellow. Balloons were used on tables and other areas for a fun atmosphere.

The families were surprised to be greeted at the front door with lively music and a costumed super hero . . .The "Head Hantscho." We had a big "H" sewn on a superman costume and our hired actor was not only big and handsome, but quite personable with the children and adults. He gave out fun futuristic gifts to everyone on their arrival. The kids were really responsive to Hantscho, following him wherever he went. When he left later in the day, he stood in an open door where a strong breeze was blowing. His cape flew up behind him, he pushed his hands forward and turned his head to this "short" audience and strongly told them to "Always Be Good!" They cheered as he left and we, as parents and event planners, were thrilled!

In addition, we had more live music during lunch. A caricature artist drew the children's faces on the top of the "Head Hantscho" body, giving them a one-of-a-kind souvenir of this special day. An exceptional magician presented exciting fun for all. They sang songs together, the owner thanked them for their participation and all went home happy . . . including the client, our vendors and Master of Ceremonies staff. Good job!

Chapter
20

Publicity
and the
Special Event

CHAPTER 20

PUBLICITY AND THE SPECIAL EVENT
How to Capture the Promotional Spotlight

Often one of the major advantages of having a special event is the ability to get publicity presented through news media — television, radio and newspapers. No matter what the ultimate purpose of the event — creating awareness of something, raising funds for a good cause, or pure private enterprise, free publicity goes a long way toward accomplishing your goals. Publicity considerations are so important that you may want to time your event so that media exposure is maximized.

In some cases, publicity itself is the goal of the event, such as when a commercial product is being introduced, or when a specific idea is being launched. On such occasions, steps must be taken to ensure media coverage. One good way to accomplish this is to have dignitaries or celebrities at your event. Politicians nearly always attract the press.

Planning Your Publicity

No matter what the special event, the public relations planner must research and know the company, or the sponsoring organization, in a thorough, reliable manner. A few areas to study include annual reports and historical documents, and talking to people that have been there a long time. If you are handling the publicity and have not been involved with the actual planning of the special event, it would be best to talk with manangement early on, to become familiar with the overall purpose of the event and what it hopes to accomplish.

The more information you have collected, the better job you can do in writing a thorough news release. You will need to be very creative when you sit down to write your release. The competition for

Dignitaries add credibility and increase publicity potential to special events. An auto dealer's dedication earned extensive attention through political attendance.

space in the newspaper and air time on television is fierce. For that reason, a unique angle that you might create could get you just the response you are hoping for from the media.

If you do not have a formal media list, contact your Chamber of Commerce, or go through your local Public Relations Society. One of the two sources will produce media lists, often free for the asking.

If the above fails, then research the local media — where do you read business stories of the type you are preparing? Simply call each and ask which editor you should send your release to, or if it is a television or radio station, call the news department and ask for the person who assigns reporters to events. You should also inquire about the deadline times for news broadcasts and the various newsprint possibilities. This information can help you plan the time of your event to maximize the opportunities for media coverage.

In print media, try to interest the local editor in the photo possibilities of your event. He will possibly assign a reporter *and* a photographer to the story.

If yours is a national or international company or group, you will also want to include the national sources of communication, such as the Associated Press and United Press International on your press release list.

Press releases should also be sent to the appropriate industry publications that run these kinds of stories. It will be helpful to send photographs to these magazines. I recommend black and white pictures with captions typed, cut out and attached to the back of the photograph with clear tape. These magazines, as well as some of the local newspapers, may print your story word-for-word, so give consideration to that and write the press release in as journalistic a manner as possible. This can be an advantage to getting the coverage you want.

In all cases, when writing a news release, keep it brief and to the point. You will be answering their questions — who, what, where, when, why and how. This needs to be done in as interesting a form as possible, but creativity is not as important as clarity. Make sure your facts are specific and accurate.

The news release for an event should be sent out at least two weeks prior to the event. The week of the event it is acceptable to call to inquire if someone will be assigned to the story. This is a good time for you to use verbal enthusiasm to peak their interest.

When the press arrives at your event, greet them with an offer of assistance, including an introduction to top management. Have a fact sheet prepared and available for them to take back to their office to help in writing the story. Fact sheets are just what they sound like — details surrounding the event, the organization, its goals and management and the goals of the event.

If you have had success with getting your story in the newspaper or on television, a quick note of thank you for their professionalism, etc. to the reporter is acceptable. But that is all — and the purpose of that is to maintain a good communication level, in the event that you want to do it again sometime.

There is never any assurance that all of the phone calls and well-written press releases will get the attention of the media. However, the possibilities are very good that you will have some success, and the time investment will definitely be worth it.

Press Release Sample

The following press release was produced for a printing company that was celebrating its anniversary. An open house was planned for invited guests and dignitaries.

The end result of this effort was that a community newspaper reporter visited the plant the day before this event and wrote a feature story on our client and the company. In addition, the city newspaper photo editor covered the event. A picture of the running press, with open house guests looking on, was printed on the front page of the business section.

Television coverage included segments on two network stations' evening newscasts for a total of four and one-half minutes. Both stations interviewed management and went on the plant tour. They filmed people running the presses, the attendees watching and a strong positive statement was the result. Sometimes you hit a "home run," and it's worth all the effort you put into the game!

PRESS RELEASE

FOR FURTHER INFORMATION CONTACT:
Bonnie Niccolls
XYZ Printing Company
407 Main Street
Lousiville, Kentucky 40202
Phone: 502-333-3333   June 13, 1991
                                FOR IMMEDIATE RELEASE

AMERICAN PRINTING CELEBRATES
25 YEARS OF PRINTING AT ITS BEST

American Printing, for 25 years a full-service printing company located at 333 Beechnut Pass, will celebrate 25 years of "Printing At Its Best." In conjunction with the celebration, the new Heidelberg press will be unveiled. This new computerized press from West Germany, will give American Printing state-of-the-art capabilities in the printing industry, including unique quality control inking, printing and high productivity.

President J. D. Sanderling noted that " . . . in the next few years, American Printing will be spending one million dollars on technological advances." The company's growth has attracted much attention, including the 1990 Industry Growth Award. Recently, American Printing received outstanding vendor awards from 7 local and national clients.

Sanderling attributed the company's success to the dedication and longevity of its employees. "We feel a social responsibility as well as a business responsibility to the local community. In return, the community has given us good people," Sanderling stated.

The Open House Celebration is scheduled for January 14, 1990, from 5:00 until 7:30 p.m. Tours, demonstrations of the new press, and a commemorative ceremony at 5:45 p.m. will highlight the event.

- 30 -

Media List

A sample press/media list follows. It was developed by researching the publications that a business audience would routinely read and television broadcasts they would watch. The selected publications and broadcast stations were called to find out to whom the press release should be sent. The addresses and phone numbers were also secured. Deadlines were researched as well as any special requests for receiving press releases. Such a list requires updating every six months:

Press List - Updated 5/24/90

WORS - TV 7   Jack Jeffries
P.O. Box 7231   News Director
Louisville, KY 40232
333-4044

WALL - TV 31   David Vaughn
333 Main Street   Assignment Editor
Louisville, KY 40203
444-0888

WZAZ - TV 18   Peggy Cook
P.O. Box 222   Assignment Editor
Louisville, KY 40201
341-1111

WOOP - TV 21   Darlene Brennan
P.O. Box 8844   Program Director
Louisville, KY
349-8777

WZZX - TV 28   Pat Wiley
P.O. Box 4444   Assignment Editor
Louisville, KY 40202   Pat Maziorkas
777-7700   Weekend Editor

Choice Cable
111 Thrift Drive
Louisville, KY 40208
444-4021

Mary Ann Johnson
Program Director

Powerline
P.O. Box 73
Louisville, KY 40203
384-4333

Mary Otting
Editor

The "Sizzlers"
P. O. Box 820
Louisville, KY 40207
589-3333

Judy Sacra
Photographic Editor

The Legend
404 73rd Street
Louisville, KY 40202
407-5333

Malinda South
Business Editor

Diane McChesney
Asst. Business Editor

Carol Welker
"Neighborhoods"

Associated Press
324 W. Maple
Louisville, KY 40202
884-8444

Billy Scott
Chief of Bureau

United Press International
333 S. Second Street
Louisville, KY 40202
588-8880

Doris Higdon
Bureau Chief

Publicity Checklist

Determine goals: Media coverage to be local, national,
                          international
               Professional publications
               Press events
               Personal appearances on TV or radio

Update media list: Best days of week
               Best time of day

Press release: Interview management
               Write press release
               Send to media list
               Follow-up with phone calls

Media events: Determine date, time and place
               Send invitations
               Arrange sound system and photo-
                         graphic area with electricity
                         and telephone
               Brief management/spokesperson
               Allow for security if necessary

Press kits: Assemble copies of speeches
               Copies of program for events,
                         speaker bios, fact sheet of
                         organization

Send thank you notes:

Evaluate results: What to continue or change for best
                   results

Chapter
21

Legal Aspects and
Insurance Needs of
Special Events

CHAPTER 21

LEGAL ASPECTS AND INSURANCE NEEDS OF SPECIAL EVENTS
Producing it Safe - A Review of Responsibilities

This chapter will be short and to the point. The host is ultimately liable for the people at his event. Therefore, my advice to all event hosts is to get adequate legal counsel and insurance protection.

Any time one hosts a number of people, either on his own property or at a rented facility, one assumes liability for what could happen to those people. If something should happen and an injury occurs, regardless of who is originally responsible, the host is ultimately liable.

There are some obvious ways a host can take precautions to avoid problems.

Some of the safety tips to know and check in advance are:

— Handicapped requirements
— Medical contacts/facilities in the area and the appropriate telephone number
— Emergency exits in the facility
— CPR training of staff
— First aid station
— Fire alarms in each room
— Evacuation procedures

Always call your attorney and your insurance person. Tell them *exactly* what you are planning, in detail, to be sure you have adequate insurance and legal protection to cover your organization. Your insurance person may advise added insurance coverage — a rider or an umbrella policy just for this event. This is a small price to pay for your confidence and level of comfort, and you will be able to concentrate more clearly on the objectives of your event.

Your attorney, if you call prior to any contract signings, may want to assist in the wording of your contracts. For example, he may identify some financial fees you may be responsible for if an unforeseen happening occurs, that you may have missed.

The best approach to any unpleasant possibilities is "Risk Management."

Risk management consists of:

— Searching out potential problems and fixing them to the best of your ability
— Retaining close control of the elements and vendors involved
— Being sure your insurance coverage is adequate
— Reviewing your event with your attorney

A contract with your vendors is best written in common language, so that everyone understands it clearly. It is a "road map" for your successful event — everyone knows exactly where to go and what to expect when they get there. The advantage of a contract can be seen in the following scenario:

A contract clearly states the date, time, place and method of payment for an event. If the musical group shows up to play an hour late at this event, due to *their* misunderstanding, and you no longer want them to play and do not wish to pay them, you have only to point to the contract. If a fair musician's union is involved, they will support *you*, because the contract spelled it out in black and white.

Alcohol is uppermost on all of our minds today. The host of an event should be well aware of his responsibility in the provision of alcohol. The Dram Shop Law strictly imposes criminal liability if one serves alcohol to someone who is already intoxicated or is a minor. This law is practically nationwide today.

The host's ethical responsibility is to prevent an intoxicated individual from driving away from the event.

Some easy ways to accomplish this are:

— Offer to drive them home
— Ask someone else to take them home
— Give them a place to "sleep it off"

— Call them a cab

Beyond the legalities of alcohol consumption, there are other tips for controlling such situations. They are:

— Shorten your cocktail "hour"
— Be sure there is plenty of food available for your guests to eat
— Protein appetizers, such as cheese, shrimp and chicken, are especially helpful
— Don't serve too many salty snacks; they make people thirsty and they will drink more
— Have waiters circulating around the room offering hors d'oeuvres while people are drinking
— Do not have circulating waiters refilling drinks
— Station the bar away from the door in a less accessible place, so people are not always passing it
— Hire a professional bartender and insist he/she use a jigger to measure alcohol and to keep it light
— Close the bar an hour before the event ends and serve pastries, coffee and milk
— Have your dinner wine poured rather than placing the bottle on the table
— Place water, soda and ice stations around the room, so that people can easily freshen their drinks without adding more alcohol
— Feature an exotic non-alcoholic drink, something that is perhaps part of the theme
— Think about limiting the bar to beer and wine; this should keep most drinkers happy, and will make things simpler
— Give attendees drink tokens or tickets; this will quietly establish a sense of how many drinks a person ought to have; you can make the bar a cash bar with non-alcoholic drinks offered free
— Don't turn the lights down too low; it encourages people to drink more and cuts down on active socializing
— Don't have the music too loud, it makes it difficult for

people to talk, driving them to drink instead of conversation
— After a meal, sometimes mineral water instead of brandy or
coffee is good; a great amount of control can be established
with your own attitude about drinking

These are only suggestions for you to consider based on industry practices and common sense. I offer them to help you with guidelines and possible solutions. I am not a specialist in the many laws that could possibly affect a special event or its sponsor. In fact, I want to be "held harmless" in my discussion of legal issues. I do know that many laws are a matter of great importance in the special events business. If you follow any of the above suggestions, be sure to include the advice of an attorney, and upon his judgement, obtain insurance coverage for the many liability areas that occur.

Chapter
22

Finale

CHAPTER 22

FINALE

My company's philosophy towards special events is very much like this book — to "create events within the event" or "creating a surprise while producing a spectacle." I have described how to create, organize and manage events of all types, while giving examples of those messages through the case studies.

It has been my mission to not only describe "what-to" and "how-to," but to develop the attitude toward creativity, quality and professionalism that is necessary to have a successful promotional event . A successful event will always produce a good return on your investment.

As business savvy expands in the new decade, and marketing becomes more finely focused, special events have risen to new heights of utilization and effectiveness. Event promotions are side by side with advertising and public relations as part of a marketing mix. The industry has mushroomed dramatically because of its one-on-one communications capability.

The stature of special events as a marketing tool, as a strong industry and as a profession has been declared in such publications as *Money* magazine, in the June 1990 issue. The top 15 careers for the 90s were profiled. The entry,"Special Events Marketer," was described as follows:

"The corporate search for cost-effective ways to reach niche markets and stand apart from the competition has made special events one of the fastest growing areas in marketing. In just five years, as the number of corporations pinning their names on special events has risen from 1,600 to 3,800, the industry has grown from $850 million to $2.1 billion. That means there will be a big demand for the specialists who plan, promote and produce corporate sponsored sporting events, festivals and cultural extravaganzas.

"As a rule, special events marketers work for an independent events agency with many corporate clients, for a company such as Anheuser-Busch or A T & T with an in-house events department, or for an advertising agency. Getting ahead requires working your way up from pre-event preparations to directing events. Tasks along the way can include promoting the event with the media, negotiating contracts with technicians and stars, and on-site management.

"All the celebrities and media attention can make events marketing intoxicating. But there is a flip side to the glamour: a flurry of last-minute preparations for each event often means eighteen hour days for a week or two at a stretch. But many thrive on the hectic pace." Says Richard Adler, who manages four tennis events a year for ProServ, an Arlington, Virginia sports marketing and management firm, "The adrenaline rush is unbelievable."

Business Opportunities '90s says event planning services "is the hottest new addition to the service industry."

"A lot of careful planning goes into making an event successful and most individuals and companies simply do not have the time or the manpower to make the plans themselves. That's why they're paying for the services of event planners.

These behind-the-scenes organizers schedule every aspect of an event, from what time the speaker takes the platform at a convention to what time the bride and groom cut the cake at their reception. And none of this is arbitrary — a lot of psychology and common sense goes into creating a successful event.

Event planning is a very versatile business that allows you to coordinate a variety of events or to specialize in one area. If you loved planning your own wedding and have helped your sisters, friends or cousins plan theirs, you might want to specialize in wedding planning. For individuals who have a lot of business sense, the corporate market could be just the target for you. Most planners agree that the corporate market represents the greatest potential for profits since corporations often need an event planner's services on an ongoing basis."

All this means that special events are definitely a part of the future of business. Special events are multi-faceted, to say the least, and therefore require thorough execution to maximize their positive potential.

The many guidelines set forth in this book will assist you in accomplishing success. I urge that you listen to my concerns for creativity — therein lies the uniqueness that will cause your guests to carry memories beyond the event, and share them in future professional situations, giving you this greater return on your investment.

I also want to reiterate that often — most often — events are too large, too detailed and multi-faceted for the non-professional. Call on a professional special events firm to ensure your success. Sometimes to the part-time planner, special events are looked upon simply as "fun." This attitude does not bring about the kind of professional results that positively affect a company's bottom line.

A professional event planner knows where to go to get the best for your function. This does not mean the most expensive; indeed, a professional knows where *not* to spend excessive money. It means value — where to get the most for your investment. Events are high ticket expenditures. They must be handled wisely — as wisely as your company would handle any other expense.

Your special events professional will follow codes of ethics and standards as set forth in the Bylaws of The International Special Events Society. ISES is a professional association that protects and insures that the member special events firms will produce promotions of quality.

If your position in your company is Chief Executive Officer, Assistant to the C.E.O., Public Relations Director, Human Resources Manager, Sales Manager or the "Host with the Most," or if in your association you are the Executive Director, Administrative Assistant or on the Board of Directors, I say that you have made the right decision to invest in special events promotion by reading this book. Congratulations on your interest in this "now" medium. It is tremendously exciting to see an industry skyrocket as special events has done right before all of our eyes. Special events momentum will continue forward as time repeatedly proves their effectiveness.

As President of Master of Ceremonies and a professional special events producer, I open my doors to my readers for further communication. If I personally can be of any assistance to a sincere interest in special events promotions, call me. I am in Louisville, Kentucky — city of *powerful women, pretty horses and spectacular events!*

Call on me . . . and remember to COLOR YOUR SPECIAL EVENTS WITH CREATIVITY!

GLOSSARY

AGENDA — A written and established schedule giving time and sequence of topics and sessions at a meeting; often includes room or location and names of speakers, moderators and other program participants.

AIR-COOLED LASER — A high intensity air lamp creating laser-like beams operating on a standard 115 VAC, cooled by air; used for indoor presentations, primarily safe for an audience scan effect.

AMERICAN PLAN — Overnight room accommodations which include three meals a day.

ATTENDEE — Individual attending the meeting sessions.

AUDIOVISUAL (AV) — Materials and equipment using sound and images for presentations.

AUTHORIZED SIGNATURE — Signature of person with authority to charge for an organization.

B LIGHTS — A string of 35 to 100 half-watt miniature lights spaced 8" apart; sometimes referred to as mini- or Italian lights.

BACKDROP — Drapes at the back of a stage, dais or exhibit booth.

BACK LIGHT — Stage lighting that projects from the rear of an object.

BACKSTAGE — The portion of the theater behind the main curtain.

BANNER — A horizontal or vertical rectangular sign carrying a message for a convention, meeting, etc.

BAR READING — A detailed written record of liquor consumption during an event.

BLEACHERS — A covered or uncovered stand of tiered seating space for spectators of events.

BLEED — Ink that runs to edge of paper when printing.

BLOCK — Number of rooms held for a group for a specified period of time.

BLOCKING — The manner and time in which a director sets up the action for a production.

BLUELINE — Final proof of printed copy for client's approval before printing.

BOOK — To definitely commit space or entertainment.

BOOM MICROPHONE — A microphone attached to a long movable arm.

BREAKOUT SESSIONS — Small group sessions within the meeting, formed to discuss specific subjects.

BREAKS — Refreshment periods between sessions, where attendees can move from one session to another.

BUTLER SERVICE — A method of serving by waiters walking around passing food and drinks to guests.

BY THE BOTTLE — Liquor served and charged for by the full bottle.

BY THE DRINK — Liquor served and charged for by the number of drinks served.

BY THE PIECE — Food priced by the individual piece.

CABARET TABLE — A small table, fifteen to thirty inches in diameter.

CALL BRAND — A brand of liquor requested by a customer.

CAPTAIN — The person responsible for service at banquet functions.

CARTAGE — Short-haul moving of exhibits for trade shows.

CASH BAR — A bar setup that allows guests to pay for their own drinks.

CENTER POLES — The poles used to support the center, and highest, part of a tent.

CHASER — A mild drink that is consumed following hard liquor.

CHASER LIGHTS — Lights wired so that a control device can turn individual lights on and off, creating a moving pattern.

CHERRY PICKER — Equipment used to lift a person to a given height.

CHIEF FINANCIAL OFFICER (CFO)   — Individual in an organization responsible for the financial management of the company.

CLEAR-SPAN TENTS — Tents with an aluminum frame support that supports the canvas, eliminating center tent poles.

CLINIC — A hands-on workshop type of educational experience where students can learn or improve skills by doing.

COMBO — A small musical ensemble, usually three to five musicians.

COMMISSIONABLE — Type of sale in which a fee, or percentage of the amount of sale, is to be paid to the agent or purchaser.

COMPLIMENTARY — Service, space or item received without charge.

CONCURRENT SESSIONS — Sessions on a variety of topics scheduled at the same time.

CONFERENCE — Participatory meeting designed for discussion of subjects related to a specific topic or area. May include fact finding, problem solving and consultation.

CONFERENCE-STYLE SETUP — Tables set in a rectangular or oval shape with chairs on both sides and ends.

CONTINENTAL BREAKFAST — Light morning refreshment, usually juices, pastries and hot beverages.

CONTINGENCIES — Promises made in agreements or contracts that can be affected by future uncertainties.

CONTRACT — A legal and binding agreement between two or more parties.

CONVENTION—Assemblage of delegates, representatives and members of an organization convened for a common purpose.

CONVENTION BUREAU — Service organization that provides destination promotion, booking, and services, including convention personnel and housing.

CONVENTION SERVICES MANAGER — Employee of a facility or hotel who is responsible for the facility related details of an event.

CORDIAL — A sweet alcoholic liqueur, often served after dinner.

CORDLESS MICROPHONE — A portable microphone which operates on its own power source.

CORKAGE — A charge placed on alcoholic beverages brought into a facility but purchased elsewhere.

CORNER BOOTH — Exhibit space with aisles on two sides.

CUE — A signal to indicate a predetermined action.

CUE CARD — A card used by performers to assist in reading or remembering lines.

DAIS — A riser on which the head table is positioned.

DANCE FLOOR — A portable area for dancing can be rented and assembled for events.

DATA BASE — Collection of historical information to be used for current or future planning.

DECORATOR — General contractor or service contractor, usually hired to set up an exhibition.

DELEGATE — A voting representative at a meeting.

DESTINATION MANAGEMENT COMPANY (DMC) — A company, based where a meeting is being held, that can handle activities, ground transportation and themed events.

DIE-CUTTING — Process of cutting shapes into a sheet of printed stock.

DIMMER — A device used to create lighting effects.

DRAYAGE — Transfer of exhibit booths, equipment, materials and properties from point of arrival to exhibit site.

DUOTONE — Photograph prepared for two-color printing.

EASEL — A three-legged stand with a rack used to hold posters, flipcharts or signs.

EPERGNE — A pedestal used for floral arrangements or other focal points.

EVENT ORDER — Detailed instructions for an event.

EXHIBIT BOOTH — Individual display area constructed to exhibit products or promote a service.

EXHIBIT HALL — Area within the facility where exhibits are located.

EXHIBIT PROSPECTUS — Promotional materials and published specifications, rules and regulations for prospective exhibitors. It is designed to encourage participation.

EXHIBITION MANAGER — Person responsibile for all aspects of an exhibition or trade show.

EXHIBITOR'S KIT — Information and request forms prepared and sent by decorator to all registered exhibitors.

FEEDBACK — Sound traveling from speakers back through a microphone, which causes uncomfortable squealing sounds.

FLAT RATE — One price, based on average cost, for all guest/ sleeping rooms in a hotel.

FLIPCHART — A large pad of paper placed on an easel, used for illustration by speakers at meetings.

FLOOR PLAN — The physical layout of a room, including dimensions, to assist in developing event plans.

FOAM CORE — Two sheets of lightweight coated paper with a styrofoam center, used for signs, decorating and exhibits.

FOIL-STAMPING — Metallic or colored "foil leaf" used in stamping. Heat and pressure are used to print the design on a surface.

FOLLOW SPOTLIGHT — A survival spotlight that swivels, allowing the operator to follow the movement of a performer or person in the audience.

FORCE MAJEURE CLAUSE — A clause in a contract which limits a performer's liability in the need of cancellation due to circumstances beyond the artist's control.

FOUR-COLOR SEPARATION — Process of printing a full-color image, using four screened patterns from which printing plates can be engraved.

FOUR-HOUR CALL — Usual minimum work period for which union labor must be paid.

FRENCH SERVICE — Banquet waiters wear white gloves to serve guests.

FRONT-SCREEN PROJECTION — Projection of film from the audience side of a light reflecting screen.

FUNCTION BILL — Check or bill prepared by the hotel stating the charges for each event or function.

GERB — A pyrotechnic device that displays an approximate 2" to 2' flame.

GIVEAWAYS (OR NOVELTIES) — An item imprinted with a logo or an event theme for guests to take home to enhance the memory of the event message.

GOBO — A metal template that, on a lighting fixture, is used to project a desired pattern, such as a logo or scenery.

GROSS SQUARE FEET — The width multiplied by the length of the area.

GROUP RATE — Negotiated guest/sleeping room rate for a group.

GUARANTEED NUMBER — Those servings, meals or rooms requested and paid for regardless of whether they are actually consumed or occupied.

HALF-ROUND SETUP — A 60" to 72" round table with people seated only around the half of the table facing the speaker or stage.

HALFTONE — Photograph that has been prepared for a single-color reproduction.

HANDOUTS — Materials given to attendees at sessions that were not included in the registration packets.

HEAD COUNT — The actual number of guests at an event.

HEAD TABLE — The most visible area to seat VIPs and the emcee at a function.

HONORARIUM — Voluntary payment made for services that require no fee.

HOSPITALITY SUITE — Large room or suite used to entertain guests.

HOUSE BRAND — An established brand of alcohol used by a facility to assist a lower budget.

HOUSE LIGHTS — Standard in-house lighting separate from the stage lighting.

HOUSE WINES — The standard wines offered by a facility, usually at lower cost.

ICE CARVING — A decorative piece carved from a large block of ice for a food table centerpiece.

INCIDENTALS — All expenses, other than room and tax, billed to a guest's account, such as room service and telephone calls.

INCLUSIVE — Catering or accommodation rates that include gratuities and taxes.

INDEMNIFICATION — Protection from liability under stated circumstances or exemption from incurred liabilities.

INDUSTRIAL SHOW — An exhibit of numerous related or similar products by various companies for the purposes of introducing new products, sales promotion and increased visibility to the general public.

KEG — A bulk container for beer or wine, usually affords better pricing.

LASER — A light mechanism that produces an intense ray of piercing color, brilliant light about one-eighth inch in diameter.

LAVALIER MICROPHONE — A portable, monodirectional microphone that can attach to a speaker to allow him freedom and mobility.

LECTERN — A stand that holds a speaker's text.

LOAD-IN, LOAD-OUT — Scheduled times for the crew to load and unload equipment.

MAITRE D´ — The manager in charge at a restaurant or catered event.

MARKET — The potential consumer group likely to be interested in, or to need, a service or product.

MARQUEE — A long and narrow tent without sides.

MASK — A drape used to cover certain areas of an event from the view of the audience.

MASTER ACCOUNT — An organization's charge account for expenses incurred during a designated hotel stay.

MASTER OF CEREMONIES — Formal title for the person who presides over a program or dinner.

MICROPHONE — The basic instrument that provides the primary input for all sound systems.

MINIMUM — The smallest number of people for a function before a surcharge is applied.

MODERATOR — Person who presides over panels and forums.

MULTIMEDIA — The utilization in one program of two or more audiovisual medias.

OPEN BAR — A bar setup in which drinks are paid for by a host.

OVERHEAD PROJECTOR — A light projector that produces and magnifies an image onto a vertical screen from a horizontal transparency below.

OVERSET — Number of places set for a food event in addition to the guaranteed amount.

PANEL — Format for discussion by a moderator and two or more program participants.

PAR LIGHTS — Parabolic Aluminized Reflector lights.

PERFORMANCE BOND — Guarantee that a facility will meet all contractual specifications.

PER PERSON — An allowance of food and/or beverages purchased for an expected attendance.

PIN BEAM — A small, 25-watt lamp that projects a narrow beam of light up to 20', often used for centerpieces, mirror balls and other decor elements.

PIPE AND DRAPE — A configuration of poles supported by heavy metal bases on which support drapes are hung.

PIT — A sunken area in front of a stage that houses the musical group of a production.

PLACE CARD — A small card with an individual's name which is placed at that person's determined seat at a meal function.

PODIUM — A platform for a speaker.

POLE DRAPES — Fabric draped to hide the poles of a tent.

POST-CONVENTION BRIEFING — Meeting between the planne rand key hotel staff after the event is over to critique the meeting.

PRE-FUNCTION SPACE — An area outside the main area where an event is being held. Receptions or registration usually take place here.

PRE-CONVENTION BRIEFING — Meeting with planner, hotel department heads and key suppliers to review details of the upcoming event.

PREMIUM BRAND — The higher price brands of liquor.

PREP AREA —   The preparation area for food, usually hidden from the guests' view.

PRESENTER — Person discussing and explaining a given topic in an information session.

PRE-SET — The placement of food on tables prior to the formal seating of guests.

PRESS CONFERENCE —   A collective interview granted to the media. This is often an event itself, where refreshments can be served, etc.

PRESS GALLERY — An area set aside for photographers to get an unobstructed view of an event, as well as an adequate power supply.

PRESS KIT — A collection of background material on a newsworthy subject of timely interest which can include biographies, in-depth information reports, past press releases, production samples and clippings and is sent before an event to the media.

PRESS PASS — An identification symbol that allows free, unrestricted entry to an event by media personnel.

PRESS RELEASE — A written message of news which is timely and sent to targeted medium, answering the questions within the first paragraph.

PRESS ROOM — An area, or room, close to an event with telephones and office machines that are made available to identified media representatives.

PROCEEDINGS — Official transcript of the program content, usually written and bound.

PRODUCER — The person responsible for the entire event program.

PROGRAM BOOK — Printed schedule of meeting events, function room locations, and other pertinent information.

PROGRAM DESIGN — Structure of meeting program elements to achieve meeting goals and objectives. Includes presentation method, topics, special events, free time and breaks.

PROOF — Final copy of printed material for approval before printing.

PROPERTY — Lodging establishment such as a hotel, conference center or meeting facility.

PROPS — The stage furniture and all articles used by entertainers on stage.

PROSPECTUS — Facility data and meeting specifications submitted to prospective clients.

PSA's — Public Service Announcements; free commercial space given by the media to non-profit organizations as available.

PUBLICITY — Information with news value issued as a means of gaining attention or support.

PUBLIC RELATIONS — A management function that evaluates public attitudes, identifies the policies and procedures of an individual or an organization with public interest, and plans and executes a program of action to earn public understanding and acceptance.

PYROTECHNICS — The art of making and using fireworks such as rocket flares and smoke bombs.

RACK RATE — Hotel's standard guest/sleeping room rate.

RAIN DATE — Another show date, contracted for in case of rain.

RECEPTION — A relatively short social function where food and drinks are served.

REFRESHMENT BREAK — A period between meeting sessions when coffee and/or other refreshments are served.

RISERS — Portable platforms of varying height assembled together to create a stage.

ROPE LIGHTS — A string of small, low-voltage lights inside a clear or colored transparent plastic tube run by a controller.

ROSTRUM — A speaker's platform.

ROUGH LAYOUT — Sketchy or tentative rendering of approximate placement of art and type for printing or meeting room setup.

ROUND — A round banquet table; 60" and 72" in diameter are most frequently used.

RUNNER — A long, narrow carpet down an aisle or onstage.

SCHOOLROOM SETUP — Tables and chairs arranged in designated rows that face the front of the room.

SCORE — A written copy of musical composition showing all of the parts of the instruments or voices.

SELF-CONTAINED — An entertainment act, group or production that can supply its own equipment.

SEMINAR — Lecture or dialogue in which participants share experiences under the guidance of a discussion leader.

SERPENTINE SETUP — Tables arranged in curving shapes, appearing to be an S.

SERVICE LEVEL — Types of coverage and quality of services offered by a facility or contractor.

SHOT — A one ounce measurement of liquor.

SIDE WALLS — Detachable canvas or plastic walls to be used to create the sides of a tent.

SINGLE — One musician or performer.

SOUND EFFECTS — Sounds created for special theatrical effect.

SOUNDSCAPING — A composition of recorded audio that creates a special environment.

SOUND SYSTEM — An electric audio speaker system, used to produce sound.

SPECIAL-RATE PACKAGE — A lowered, all-inclusive rate, frequently including one or more meals for two-three nights, that is offered to the general public and is often used to generate off-season or weekend business.

SPECIFICATIONS — Complete description of meeting requirements, ususally written.

SPOKESPERSON — A representative who has the knowledge and credibility to speak to and be intereviewed by the media.

SPONSORSHIP — Limited sponsor for an event, which in turn allows promotion of that organization or company that assumes a specified financial responsibility.

SPOTLIGHT — A strong beam of light used to illuminate a particular person or object.

STACKING CHAIRS — Chairs that will save space by stacking on top of each other.

STAGE CALL — A notice to performers to gather at a cerain time and place for a review of responsibilities.

STAGE LIGHTING — The lighting used to illuminate a stage.

STAGE RIGHT, STAGE LEFT — A description of directions for performers or those involved in a production.

STAKES — Wooden or steel pointed pegs used to secure the guy ropes of a tent in the ground.

STANCHIONS — Upright bars, or posts, with ropes attached to define areas at gatherings.

STANDING MICROPHONE — A microphone attached to an adjustable stand on the floor.

STRIKE — To remove all scenery and props, or to dismantle and remove an exhibit.

STORYBOARD — A series of rough sketches that give direction to planning a program.

STROBE LIGHTS — An electronic lighting instrument that emits extremely rapid but brief flashes of brilliant light.

SUPPLIER — Facility, company, agency or person supplying space, goods or services.

SYMPOSIUM — Event at which experts discuss a particular subject and opinions are expressed.

TABLE WINE — Wines naturally fermented at approximately 14 percent alcohol.

TALENT — Entertainers or performers used in a production.

T & T — An abbreviation used to signal tax and tip.

TECHNICAL DIRECTOR — A trained individual who calls for cues for a performance.

TELECONFERENCE — Type of meeting that brings together three or more people in two or more locations through telecommunications.

TELEPROMPTER — An electronic device which the audience cannot see that displays a magnified script to aid a speaker or performer.

THEATER SETUP — Chairs placed in rows facing the front of the room.

THEME BREAK — Break during formal program sessions with special foods and beverages pertaining to a theme, sometimes including decorations, costumes and entertainment.

TIME AND MATERIALS — Method of charging for services and materials used on a cost-plus basis.

TOWER — A structure used to hold lighting equipment above a performance area.

TRACK LIGHTING — Lights attached to a metal track mounted on a ceiling or wall, allowing flexible spotlighting.

TRADE SHOW — Exhibition of products and services that may or may not be open to the public. When associated with a meeting, this type of show is often only open to registered attendees.

TRANSPARENCIES —   A transparent plastic sheet or roll, clear or colored, that provides the image projected from an overhead projector to a screen.

TRUSS — A structure of steel bars used to suspend lighting or other technical equipment over a stage.

TURNOVER — The time required to break down and reset a function room.

U-SHAPED SETUP — Chairs arranged in a U shape that face the head table or speaker.

VARIETY ENTERTAINMENT — Singers, dancers, comics or other stand-up performers.

VELOX — Photographic material used in preparing camera-ready art; a high contrast black-and-white proof.

VIP (Very Important Person) — Organization officers, celebrity speakers, panel moderators, industry experts or others who have distinguished themselves from the majority in attendance.

WARM-UP — An activity or performance used prior to show time, to liven up or entertain the audience.

WINGS — The offstage area immediately left and right of the stage.

WORKSHOP — Training session in which participants, often through exercises and hands-on projects, develop skills and knowledge in a given field.

TENTS, SEATING CHARTS AND MISCELLANEOUS

TENT SIZES:

The following are the average tent sizes needed to accommodate the average size corporate or association events:

	STAND UP COCKTAILS	FULL SIT DOWN	SIT DOWN BUFFET
16' x 16'	45	26	35
20' x 20'	65	40	55
20' x 30'	100	60	85
30' x 30'	180	100	125
40' x 40'	350	240	280

TENT ACCESSORIES:

Fans	Clamp on Lights
Heaters	Drop Lights
Air Conditioners	Halogen Lights
Compressor/Auxiliary	Box Lights
Power Supply	Par Lights
Sidewalls w/Windows	Lattice Pole Cover
Flooring & Carpet	Greenery/Ribbons/Pole Covers
Gutters	Clear Sidewalls
Clear Tops	Dance Floors
Flags	Staging

TENT TERMS:

Party Canopy — A lightweight covering designed to shelter against the sun or light rain, usually supplied as an inexpensive do-it-yourself tent rental. Includes one or more centerpoles.

Pop-Up Canopy — A small, lightweight, collapsible frame canopy with a fabric covering. Provides shelter and protection from light rain and usually provided as a do-it-yourself rental tent which may be erected and removed quickly.

Frame Tent — A professionally installed party tent consisting of a canvas or vinyl top stretched over a metal frame and containing NO center poles.

Pole Tent — A heavy duty party tent made of canvas or vinyl supported by poles around the perimeter and in the center. Pole tents must be installed by professionals and will shelter against most bad weather.

Marquee — A long, narrow tent structure used mainly for sheltering walkways or defining an entry to a tent.

Party Canopy

A lightweight covering designed to shelter against sun or light rain, usually supplied as an inexpensive do-it-yourself tent rental. Includes one or more centerpoles.

Pop-Up Canopy

A small, lightweight, collapsible frame canopy with a fabric covering. Provides shelter and protection from light rain and is usually provided as a do-it-yourself rental tent which may be erected and removed quickly.

Frame Tent

A professionally installed party tent consisting of a canvas or vinyl top streched over a metal frame and containing NO center poles.

Pole Tent

A heavy duty party tent made of canvas or vinyl, supported by poles around the perimeter and in the center. Pole tents must be installed by professionals and will shelter against most bad weather.

Marquee

A long, narrow tent structure used mainly for sheltering walkways or defining an entry to a tent.

SPACE AND SEATING

SEATING ALLOWANCE:

Round Tables — Allow 54" between tables for chair space and food service. Divide the room area in square feet by 10 for maximum seating. Add an additional 2 square feet per person for comfort.

Oblong Tables — Allow 60" between tables for back to back seating. Divide room in square feet by 8 for maximum seating. Add 2 square feet per person for comfort.

2-1/2" from table edge is allotted for chair space.

Theatre seating (chairs in rows)   — 6 sq. ft./person

Classroom seating (table & chairs in rows)— 6 sq. ft./person

Banquet seating, oblong/rectangular   — 8 sq. ft./person

Round tables seating 10   —10 sq. ft./person

Round tables of 6, 8, or 12   —12 sq. ft./person

Cocktail parties & receptions:
  All standing   — 6 sq. ft./person
  Some seating   — 8 sq. ft./person

ADDITIONAL SPACE CONSIDERATIONS:

Dance Area	2 - 4 sq. ft./person
Bar Area	100 sq. ft.
Buffet Area (per table)	100 sq. ft.
Piano - Spinet	50 sq. ft.
Grand	100 sq. ft.
Band	100 sq. ft.

TABLE STYLES, SEATING CAPACITY and LINEN:

Cocktail Tables	24", 30", 36" Round	Seats - 2-6
Card Tables	30' x 30'	Seats - 4
Rectangular Tables	6' x 30"	Seats 6-8
	8' x 30"	Seats 8-10
Round Tables	48"	Seats 6-8
	60"	Seats 8-10
	72"	Seats 10-12
Linen	54" x 54"	30" x 30" table
	54" x 120"	6' and 8' banquet table
	90" rounds	30", 36", 48", 60" tables
	120" rounds	60", 72" tables

U-SHAPE

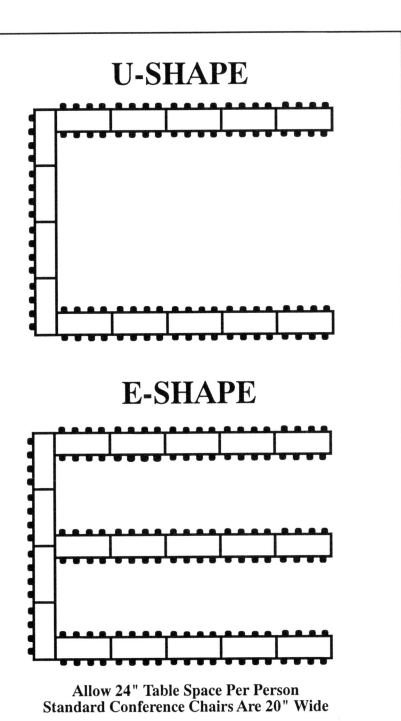

E-SHAPE

Allow 24" Table Space Per Person
Standard Conference Chairs Are 20" Wide

T-SHAPE

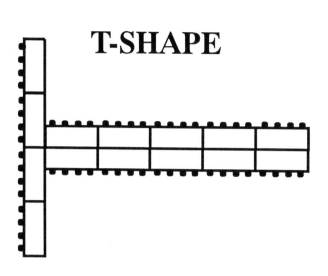

CLASSROOM

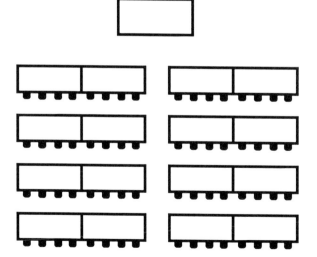

Allow 84" Between Tables

HERRINGBONE

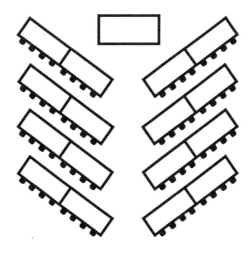

Allow 84" Between Tables

AUDITORIUM

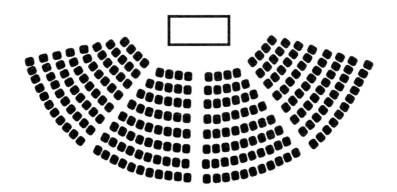

THEATRE

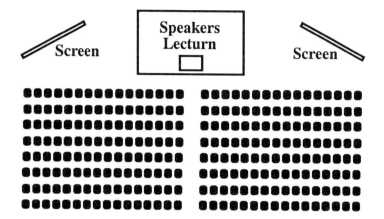

HERRINGBONE

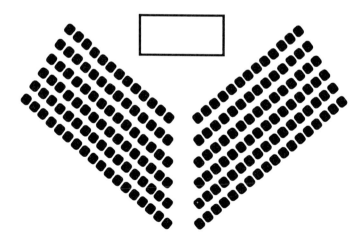

**Allow 4' For Back Aisle, 34" Between Chairs, 6' From Riser
To First Row, 4' For Center Aisle, 3' For Side Aisles**

FOOD AND BEVERAGE ALLOWANCES:

2 drinks per person per hour
2 4-oz. glasses of wine with formal dinner
1 bar for every 100 guests
1 coffee station per 60 guests
1 buffet line per 50 guests

BEVERAGES:
One keg of beer equals 160 glasses
One gallon of coffee equals 22 6-oz. cups
One fifth (25.6 oz.) equals 23 1-oz. drinks
One liter (35.6 oz.) equals 33 1-oz. drinks
One quart (32 oz.) equals 5 6-oz. glasses
One gallon of wine (64 oz.) equals 16 4-oz. glasses
One bottle of wine (24 oz.) equals 6 4-oz. glasses

HORS D'OEUVRES:
For average consumption, figure approximately 8 pieces per person. This is based on an average hors d'oeuvre buffet that includes cold food, such as fruits and cheeses, along with hot finger food.

To order additional copies of *Creating Special Events* or the audio-cassette of *Creating Special Events*, use the handy order form below.

Quantity	*Creating Special Events*	Extended Price
	Book $38.95	$
	Audio Cassette $29.95	$
	Shipping cost $3.95 per item	$
	Total Enclosed	$

Kentucky residents add 6% Sales Tax

☐ Check or money order enclosed.

☐ MasterCard ☐ VISA

Account #_____ Expiration Date _____

Cardholder Signature _____

Ship to: _____

_____

_____

_____

Phone # (day) _____

For more information please call or write:

Master Publications, Inc.
10323 Linn Station Road
Louisville, Kentucky 40223
502-426-3021

Information in this book has been gathered from hundreds of sources over many years. The following documents, articles and companies have been especially helpful resources:

AVON Information

Phillip Joel Shuman - survey on successful sponsorship

"Coping with Liquor Laws" — *The John Mossman Newsletter*

Miller Brewing Company "Responsible Event Plan" 1989

Money Magazine June 1990

New Business Opportunities 'Feb/Mar. 1989, and Oct. 1990

Entrepreneur Magazine Dec. 1990